THE PRESENT KINGDOM OF GOD

New Revised Edition

Galen Sharp

ISBN: 0994377967

ISBN-13: 978-0-9943779-6-8

The Present Kingdom Of God: New Revised Edition/ by Galen Sharp

River Of Life Publications

Printed in the United States of America

For

Barbara, Timothy and Leah

In whom the Lord delights and so do I

Acknowledgements

With appreciation to my dear friends
Ken Meeker and Scott Duncan
for their dedication and encouragement.
And a special thanks to Karla Harper and Jake Nielsen
Who were invaluable in updating this new edition

Contents

PREFACE TO THE 2016 EDITION

It has been over 40 years since the 1974 publication of "The Present Kingdom of God." Much has changed in the world and people are even more in need of the "Good News" than ever. Since the original publication, I have quietly continued living in the present kingdom of God and observed the fruition in my own life. Life is never smooth in the world, but life in the kingdom of God, resting in Christ, is the one thing that has allowed this author to thrive and to live a creative and productive life.

One day, not long ago, I was visiting with a group of dedicated Christians and, to my great surprise, several of the people in the group told me they had read the original of "The Present Kingdom of God" way back when it was available. One actually still carried his badly tattered 40 year old copy. They told me that reading it had made a deep, lasting impression on them. After discussing it, they all agreed that it has greatly liberated and empowered them and has opened them to recognize their true life in Christ and to "walking in the Spirit." It has taught and inspired them and all thought it should definitely be republished.

So, that's how I was inspired to consider this new edition. However, I was sure there were a few improvements I could make, such as better ways to present some of the information to enable readers to more easily recognize our oneness in Christ. Once deeply understood it will greatly empower and liberate the readers' Christian experience.

I welcome both new readers and those from the past to take yet another adventure into the real present kingdom of God. Much of the book remains unchanged but the new improvements should make this 2016 edition of "The Present Kingdom of God: New Revised Edition" even more accessible and more powerful for all readers.

Galen Sharp,

On a snowy day near Denver, Colorado,

February, 2016

1
An Adventure into Eternity

"The kingdom of Heaven has arrived."
Matthew 10:7 PHILLIPS

There are millions of people today who carry the silent hope that there is more to Christianity than they have been shown. They suspect that it must really be very simple, very beautiful, and wholesome. And they know that when they do see it they will immediately recognize it. That hope is real. It was given to us because there really is such a thing. Something wonderfully real, solid and awesome, just like God Himself. It is called the kingdom of God. This is not just a figurative term for something that is to be explained away in a nice compact set of rules, positive thoughts, and platitudes. Jesus Christ intends for us to actually enter into the literal kingdom of God, here and now, and to begin exploring it with Him just as His apostles first did two thousand years ago. "If it were not so, I would have told you" (John 14:2).

"Get thee out of thy country ... unto a land that I will shew thee" (Genesis 12:1). We are going on an adventure to a new "land." And, just as on any earthly adventure, we must be willing to be surprised. We must expect to encounter some strange and exotic new creatures. We will also find ourselves faced with some rather confusing and sometimes upsetting situations. We may often be discouraged and hindered by unexpected storms and difficulties. Some of our most cherished opinions might be upset, and some souls may even turn back, although we will soon find that we were never really in any danger after all, for the Chief Shepherd has been with us all along.

But unlike earthly adventures we will be embarking upon the most essential and profound journey a person can undertake. The vast peace of God will open upon us like a breath of clear air. This is a place that flesh and blood have never seen, nor even imagined. "Know the truth and the truth will set you free." (John 8:32)

This is an adventure that makes the word *adventure* sound profane. It will pierce eternity and transcend time itself. This is not a religious exercise; it is not an attainment. It is a higher realm of existence, a transformational revelation.

We can actually take the first steps simply by getting settled on just what the kingdom really is, and why we are seeking it. Jesus Himself said that it had arrived and told His disciples to announce it. Shall we begin?

What Is The Kingdom?

The kingdom of God is not something we frantically have to hold onto by the tips of our fingers. It is solid as a rock, restful, and never-changing. Nor does it involve a complex structure of intellectual truths which we must sort out and hold in our head in order to keep from falling out of it; rather, it is a realm where we can indeed live and walk.

Between the writing of the New Testament books and the present day, that realm has somehow come to be pictured as something that comes only after physical death. First we serve our time in this life, and if we have been good, then when we die we might go on to heaven. This firmly established traditional idea has been very effective in discouraging most souls at the outset in even desiring the kingdom of God, let alone seeking and discovering it. It is true that upon physical death we can come into the total experience of heaven. However, even a superficial reading of the New Testament will show that this world and God's realm are definitely *not* in a before-and-after sequence. Both are existing in the present, or we might say, parallel to each other. Both are available *now* (Hebrews 4:7-11).

Jesus even berated the Pharisees for not entering the kingdom. This shows it is available now or He wouldn't have said, "... woe unto you, scribes and Pharisees, hypocrites! For ye shut up the kingdom of heaven against men: for ye neither go in yourselves, neither suffer ye *them that are entering* to go in." Those who tell us we cannot enter the kingdom in this lifetime are no different than those Pharisees of old.

When God came to us in the flesh, He called the new realm the "kingdom of God," or the "kingdom of heaven." And He wanted to make it clear that it had, indeed, arrived. Jesus did not say, "Someday everything will get better. Just hang on now, so that when you die, things will be all right." Rather, He told His disciples to announce to the world that "the kingdom of heaven has arrived" (Matthew 10:7 PHILLIPS).

The kingdom of God is open right now! It may not yet be openly seen by all, but it is nevertheless here, and may be entered without delay. Christ warned that there was a cost, though (Luke 14:28). In fact everything of the old creation is left behind.

Christ tells us the reason for His coming was "that ye might have life and have it more abundantly" (John 10:10). He defined that life in a prayer to the Father when He said, "And this is life eternal, that they might know thee the only true God, and Jesus Christ, whom thou hast sent" (John 17:3). So we see that eternal life and the kingdom of God are not just "things" to passively possess in the future. Living in the kingdom of

God is an active, continual knowing of the person God in the present.

This may tend to sound less than exciting if we are still thinking of knowing God in the aspect of two people just conversing back and forth. Often we may feel that those conversations tend to be a bit one-sided and we are never really sure of what might be our imagination or what might really be God. But we shall soon hopefully realize that God wants us to know Him in a much more fantastic and intimate way, as a new creature created *in* Him and made *one* with Him in order to participate in *all* that He *is*. This kind of knowing is much more than we can anticipate or even imagine.

So that we might get an idea of how just knowing God could be literally synonymous with entering the new realm of existence, we will have to examine more closely our present state of existence and define a few terms. We have no doubt been promised great things before by other people, other books and advertisements, and have been badly disappointed. So it's not at all unusual to be skeptical about such far-out-sounding claims as a literal entrance into the kingdom of God. So were the people of Christ's time. And many were disappointed, but the reason is not that the kingdom was less than they had anticipated, but that it was much more incredible and vast than anything that anyone was looking for. Many either couldn't grasp it at all or, as did most, misinterpreted it and cut it down to fit their own concepts. Those people were disappointed also, but a few souls weren't. Even though the kingdom was also too much for their minds to grasp, they stuck around with Jesus long enough and the kingdom somehow grasped them! "Flesh and blood cannot reveal this unto you, but My Father which is in heaven" (Matthew 16:17).

Why don't we know God and His kingdom already? To discover the reason why we don't is also to discover the reason behind every plague and pain of human history. Let's see what happened.

Adam And Eve

Genesis 2:7 says... "The Lord God formed man from the dust of the ground, and breathed into his nostrils the breath or spirit of life and man became a living soul." Adam's spirit is the pure awareness of the Eternal Living God.

Adam was in direct awareness of the person of God. And in God was Adam's own personal *identity.* His self-awareness of being, here, now, as well as his awareness of the rest of creation was mystically linked with God's awareness. *He knew himself in and by God's own awareness of him.* His true identity was in God. Adam could know himself as he really was only in God. God is not only Himself, but he is also reality and the creator and sustainer of ALL things. Adam knew his real life in

God. Another way of saying this... man exists in God's awareness. The essential identity of Adam was divine and eternal. This identity, remember, rests in and depends on God Himself and His knowing of Adam. Since Adam's true life or identity was in God and with God, then God, rather than Adam's body and mind only, was Adam's frame of reference for every thought and action done.

The Bad News

In the third chapter of Genesis we find that something happened to drastically alter Adam's relationship with God. There have been volumes written about this catastrophe, so we couldn't hope to even partially cover its many ramifications in just a few lines. But it is very necessary to touch upon the fall of Adam and its lasting effect upon mankind so that we will be able to understand God's unique design for man's reconciliation with Him.

"Now the serpent was more subtle than any beast of the field which the Lord God had made. And he said unto the woman, Yea, hath God said, Ye shall not eat of every tree of the garden? And the woman said unto the serpent, We may eat of the fruit of the trees of the garden. But of the fruit of the tree which is in the midst of the garden, God hath said, Ye shall not

eat of it, neither shall ye touch it, lest ye die. And the serpent said unto the woman, Ye shall not surely die. For God doth know that in the day ye eat thereof, then your eyes shall be opened, and ye shall be as God, knowing good and evil. And when the woman saw that the tree was good for food, and that it was pleasant to the eyes, and a tree to be desired to make one wise, she took of the fruit thereof, and did eat, and gave also unto her husband with her; and he did eat. And the eyes of them both were opened, and they knew that they were naked; and they sewed fig leaves together, and made themselves aprons."

Genesis 3:1-7

Notice that the serpent's appeal and temptation was not made to Adam and Eve's identity in God, but to their mind and body. The serpent approached the mind and body as though it were a separate, self-existent entity in itself, disregarding their true identity, the spirit of life in God.

Now, so that we won't develop a grudge against Adam or Eve, let's remember that they, unlike you and I, were in a totally innocent state and had no self-awareness apart from God. They had never known anything but paradise and God's favor and they had nothing to compare it with. Indeed, the ability to compare good and evil was one of the serpent's offers. They had never lied and had had no experience with liars. Satan, the father of all lies, in effect was saying through the serpent, "God only lets you know what He pleases. You can know not only the things that God shows you, but also the things He is withholding, because He is jealous of what He is and doesn't want you to be like Him. He is cheating you out of the best and keeping it for Himself. Compare things for *yourself*. Then *you* will be just like God, knowing the truth and the lie. What is, as well as what is not."

Let's remember that the serpent spoke to Eve on the level of the body and mind as though she could and should be a self-existent one apart from God, the same as God. This is how Eve discovered that she could be a self-existent one apart from God, the same as God. This is how Eve discovered that she could seemingly act independently of God and her real life in Him. So, Eve with the information only from the mind and emotions made the decision to partake of the fruit. This decision was made without regard to her true spiritual identity in God, thus disobedience began. Then Adam made the same decision. When the mind turned from God and acted on its own, it was immediately submerged into the darkness of its own tiny sphere of awareness and it imagined it was an independent self separate from God. This was how the mind "created" it's own (imaginary) self as the mind and body. Adam and Eve were now in bondage to the false identity of an imaginary self, their own minds and bodies. Thus Adam and Eve were effectively shut out of paradise and barred from the Tree of Life by their actions.

Adam's fallen condition was passed to his children and then upon all mankind. We will only be in a position to realize the full implications of Adam's fall at Christ's open return; but then our thoughts will probably not be upon the old creature, but on the new-forever. Mankind's life, as it is now lived on the earth, is not lived in the glorious reality and awareness of the God who links and guides all creation in Himself, but in the feeble darkened lie of self. We now share the frustration of millions of people all futilely trying to get the universe to revolve around the tiny frame of reference "me," the body/mind.

Now maybe it is easier for us to realize how knowing God could so drastically alter our perception and how it would literally be a new realm of existence. The love and reality of the person of God and our true self in Him-loving and linking, guiding and sharing with all things in Himself. We know that God hasn't abandoned us to this fate, but has rescued us from this "delusion of a self" and has revealed to us our true identity in Him.

2
The Incredible Good News

"I come that they may have life and have it more abundantly"
John 10:10

The Way

Adam and Eve lost the knowledge of their real identity in God. After Adam, man quickly forgot that he ever had any other life except the fallen nature "me." Indeed, it wasn't long until it ceased to even enter man's mind that he might have had a real other life (identity) in God. It's not something the fallen self would be likely to think of. For such a thing to happen it would be necessary for man to leave that old identity, self, he had always known as "me." And to self that is unthinkable. Now you may be thinking, "Oh, no! I don't want to have to pretend that I am selfless." The Good News is that is not the case at all. You don't have to pretend anything anymore. I promise it will be painless, even joyous.

What kind of a life could fallen man even conceive of that would be waiting for him? So God, because He loved man and wanted him to actually see and touch this original real life in Himself and know what it was really like, sent that life to dwell with man. Now man could know that there was an alternative to the old false self: "For God so loved the world that he gave his only begotten Son, that whosoever believeth in him should not perish, but have everlasting life" (John 3:16). But even then, most misunderstood and saw that life only as a threat to their false self (indeed it was) and tried to kill it. But in doing so, man actually killed the old self he was trying to save by crucifying Christ, for "... one man died for all and therefore all mankind has died" (2 Corinthians 5:14). Thus, Christ not only showed us the true life (Himself), but in His death He liberated us from the false life (our imaginary self image, "me").

"It was there from the beginning; we have heard it; we have seen it with our own eyes; we looked upon it, and felt it with our own hands; and it is of this we tell. Our theme is the word of life. This life was made visible; we have seen it and bear our testimony; we here declare to you the eternal life which dwelt with the Father and was made visible to us."

1 John 1:1, 2 NEB

"When all things began, the Word already was. The Word dwelt with God, and what God was, the Word was. The Word, then, was with God at the beginning, and through him all things came to be; no single thing was created without him. All that came to be was alive with his life, and that life was the

light of men. The light shines on in the dark, and the darkness has never quenched it."

John 1:1-5 NEB

"He was in the world; but the world, though it owed its being to him, did not recognize him. He entered his own realm, and his own would not receive him. But to all who did receive him, to those who have yielded him their allegiance, he gave the right to become children of God, not born of any human stock, or by the fleshy desire of a human father, but the offspring of God himself. So the Word became flesh; he came to dwell among us, and we saw his glory, such glory as befits the Father's only Son, full of grace and truth."

John 1:10-14 NEB

Late one night Nicodemus, a Pharisee, sought Jesus out to inquire of Him about God's kingdom. Christ spoke to Nicodemus of two births into two different realms, saying, "Except a man be born of water [or the flesh] and of the Spirit, he cannot enter into the kingdom of God" (John 3:5).

Jesus meant that first we come into this world as natural beings, but if we are to enter the kingdom of God, we must be born over again of the Spirit of God. "That which is born of the flesh is flesh; and that which is born of Spirit is spirit" (John 3:6). This second birth is into the divine life. By natural birth we enter the race of Adam, but it is a fallen race, separated from God and in bondage to the imaginary old self. The only way to leave it is by death (but not our physical death, as we shall see). There is no other way out of the fallen Adam race.

But, through Jesus, God has provided the way out for us. Almost everyone knows that Christ died for our sins, but we still may appear to be just as bad off as before. We say, "How could that one death, so long ago, have anything to do with us now, other than make us feel sorry or guilty that such a wonderful person had to die so cruelly? So do a lot of other people die cruelly. How could He die for our sins? What exactly has that got to do with me and the kingdom of God now?"

Briefly stated, though it may not be clear yet, here is how that one death and resurrection affected all mankind, including those yet to come: all of us were included with Christ (by the Father) in Christ's death on the cross. This means that Christ's death counted for our death, also. Thus because we are "in Christ" the self image of "me" we have always known as ourselves is now counted as dead or void by the Father. That means that we have been completely released from all ties, blame, obligations, and claims to that person "me" – the false life or fallen nature that we inherited from Adam.

Then also, through Christ, we were counted by the Father to be included in the new resurrected life of

Christ. In other words, we were permanently severed from any real ties with the false self when Christ died. That left us with literally no identity or self that we could claim as ours. But when Christ rose again, God the Father counted Christ to be our true self; giving all of us the right to depend on Christ's own life to count for us, also. Since Christ ascended into heaven, we can't physically see that real life of ours, but we know what it was like because of the New Testament record of Him.

Now that *does not* mean we are just to try to copy Him or do what we think He would do. That is still depending on the false self to imitate or impersonate Christ. Nor does it mean we should try to act "selfless." No, it means that we can now depend on and live in that risen, unchangeable Life that is now with God in His kingdom, rather than be enslaved by the earthly fears, whims, vices, and frailties of the sin-dominated false life we had heretofore known as us (*see* Romans 6:5-14 NEB).

A simple understanding of these things has in itself the power to eternally alter us in such a way that we literally begin to perceive, be aware of, and know the person God, His infinite love, His glorious kingdom. But, hang on, it is totally different, yet disarmingly more familiar than any of our preconceived notions. This is the beginning of an eternal adventure.

In this book we will further explore and clarify Christ's death and resurrection in order to bring the infinite power of God contained in it into realization in our own lives.

Being born over again should not be understood only as inviting Christ into us, as is a common conception. That is a reversal of the true order of God. As we shall see presently, being born over again is a matter of our being *born into Christ* by the Holy Spirit. This happens when we are told and we understand and recognize that God (because of Christ's death and resurrection) will now reckon (or count) us as in Christ in heavenly places and in turn agree and count upon that. *Then* the Holy Spirit dwells in and makes our spirit alive unto God. That is saving faith.

As the cross is more clearly presented in the following pages we will see that it is not the old "me" that is reckoned in the resurrected Christ, or even Christ indwelling in the old "me" because there is nothing there. But instead it is a completely new self, our true self which is *hidden* in Christ in heavenly places "For ye are dead, and your true life is hid with Christ in God." (Colossians 3:3). The old false "me" that we knew (and probably still think of) as "us" was counted as crucified (made void) when Christ was crucified and no longer counts as us. As we abide in our true life in Christ in heaven, He then, by the Holy Spirit, abides in these bodies on the earth. We have not lost our identity, we have found it. Christ did not save the imaginary self image, "me," but His being is our being, our only self. "For whosoever will save his life shall lose it: and whosoever will lose his life for my sake shall find it." (Matthew 16:25). And we are then truly living because Christ *is* our new, true self, not the old imaginary "me." (Colossians3:3).

> *"I am crucified with Christ: nevertheless I live; yet not I, but Christ liveth in me: and the life which I now live in the flesh I live by the faith of the Son of God, who loved me, and gave himself for me."*
>
> *Galatians 2:20*

The modern convert, by inviting Christ into his heart, has in effect been trying to get Christ to come down and inhabit the false self or old "me" while still abiding in and identifying with this self of the old creation, he expects Christ to make it right and holy. This is something that God cannot and will not do. How can we expect the true God to agree to dwell in, give power to, and gratify the false god, our illusory "me," the lie that we have lived for as a substitute for Him ever since Adam? Unless the old self is recognized as dead and merely an intellectual thought, allowing for the new birth, the sad results of this kind of religion are no power, no honest fruit of the Spirit (only artificial), no real knowledge and fellowship with God, no clear understanding of scripture, increasing error, confusion, and frustration. He must further delude himself in order to continue in this kind of thing, thinking that deluding one's self in spite of the facts is "believing" or "having faith." He then has either a lifelong battle with sin under the law or turns to license and "backslides." That can hardly be called the kingdom of God. In any case, he always ends up secretly or openly deciding that Christianity has no power and that God falls far short of what he was expecting.

When a baby is born it is not a recycled *old* baby-it is a totally unique *new* baby. Thus it is with the new birth of a Christian. The old self or "me" that we knew as us is not cleaned up and set in heaven. Nor is it indwelt by Christ on the earth. That is not Christianity or the cross. We are not *recycled* or improved or empowered. No, something much more wonderful, we are *recreated* in Christ of (the new parent) God. "You" are a totally new creation: "... if any man be in Christ, he is a new creature: old things are passed away; behold, *all* things are become new" (2 Corinthians 5:17). Then as we rest in Christ our *hidden* (unseen to us) life in heaven, our true self Christ will then truly dwell in our spirit. The result will be true liberty, spontaneous fruit of the Spirit, honest and true fellowship with God our Father. We will once again be a complete, real person just as Adam once was.

How can these things be? We ask. We will discuss being born over again in detail later on in the book, but first let's talk a little bit more about our purpose in entering into the kingdom of God.

We see now that the kingdom is not a matter of being "religious" or doing our duty to escape hellfire. God had something very different in mind for us. He desired us as His children. He wanted us, and His purpose was that we might become complete beings as His sons and live with Him. Christ was once the only begotten (*see* John 3:16), but through His work on the cross He became the first begotten (*see* Revelation 1:5). Christ is the *first* of *many* brothers for Himself, and the *first of many* sons for the Father. It is the "new creature" of the second birth that lives and walks in the kingdom of God.

Jesus showed us that His purpose in coming was that we might have our true life in knowing God. Unfortunately, the phrase "knowing God" has been so often misused that its true meaning has been obscured. The Amplified version of the Bible expands the meaning of "knowing God:" "[For my determined purpose is] that I may know Him-that I may progressively become more deeply and intimately acquainted with Him, perceiving and recognizing and understanding [the wonders of His

Person] more strongly and more clearly" (Philippians 3:10 AMPLIFIED).

As Christians, we take for granted the assumption that we can know God and have a personal relationship with Jesus Christ. But all too often this knowing is limited either to an intellectual knowledge of Bible facts *about* Him, or to the sort of knowing one experiences in shaking hands with a new acquaintance. Or, we think of Him like we would an imaginary friend. If we have been introduced to some individual, particularly a famous person, and have had the opportunity to speak with him for a few moments, we most likely will say later that we know that person. We would say so more because it somehow seemed prestigious than because it was really true.

So it is with God: many have had a "handshake" with Him, so to speak, and have briefly spoken to Him during a religious experience. But that is where the acquaintance is left. They have met Him, they say, and would also say that they know Him. It is not that they have consciously and deliberately turned their backs upon Him but that the greeting was taken for the total. Nothing else is expected of the relationship. They were right on the threshold of the kingdom of God and never knew it!

However, in the original manuscripts of the Bible the word for *salvation* is in three tenses. These three tenses state that we were saved, are being saved, and will be saved. They cover all three aspects of our relationship in time. Thus, they are effective in expressing the eternal now of God. Our acquaintance with God is not expected to be a single experience, one lone introduction, but a *total* life. God is ever-present, and it is unthinkable that He should desire to make His presence known to us only once.

This "handshake" view of salvation makes our relationship with God a sort of unpleasant lifelong test, or a battlefield between opposing forces. The experience of becoming a Christian becomes past tense, becomes something to be only remembered. Or in some cases something one tries to forget. One's attitude degenerates into something like "Yes, that has happened to me and I am set and ready to go to heaven. All I have to do is hang on, stay in the church, and see if I can keep from backsliding until I die or get too old to sin. Maybe the rapture will come soon, or ... by and by a pie in the sky when I die!"

Let's try to put ourselves in God's position in this sort of relationship. How would we feel if our own child said to us, "Well, Dad, I suppose I am glad that you are my father, but let me tell you, being your son is no easy thing. I certainly hope I will have the determination to stick it out with you until I die, or at least until I can get out of this house and out from under all the pressure put on me here!"

Life with Christ in God does not sound very attractive when put in those terms, does it? Yet often that is exactly how we "know" God.

God did not send His son to die on the cross just to give us the burden of an impossible example to try to live up to, or just so that we could have "fire insurance" from the destruction to come! Nor is He standing with His hat in His hand, begging us not to go to hell. We were not saved so that we could just lead a good life and witness. He is Almighty God! Master of all creation! The I AM! He sent His Son because He loves us very much and desired our companionship and participation with Him. It is not possible even to begin to explain fully the kind of life and love He has for us. But it can be experienced!

And that is what He wants: for us to *experience* Him. To experience Him is also to experience His kind of love, which is so far beyond the dulled and twisted thing we normally understand as "love" that we cannot even imagine it. His kind of love is *completely* unselfish and *entirely* focused on our good. And it is not even to satisfy "God's need to love something," as some would have us believe. He is complete and satisfied in Himself. Fellowship with Him is *His desire for us,* for all of us; it is not some reward He bestows upon the super spiritual. It is not made available only for the strong-willed, but for "whosoever will" (*see* Revelation 22:7; John 3:16). We shall discover in our own experience that abiding in His love brings a solid peace and inner liberty that totally transforms our lives. It is the abundant life.

The Life

"It was there from the beginning; we have heard it; we have seen it with our own eyes; we looked upon it, and felt it with our own hands; and it is of this we tell. Our theme is the word of life. This life was made visible; we have seen it and bear our testimony; we here declare to you the eternal life which dwelt with the Father and was made visible to us. What we have seen and heard we declare to you, so that you and we together may share in a common life, that life which we share with the Father and his Son Jesus Christ. And we write this in order that the joy of us all may be complete."

1 John 1:1-4 NEB

When Jesus saw Martha mourning the death of Lazarus (John 11:1-44), He told her that Lazarus would rise again. Martha said that she knew this would happen at some point in the future, on the last day. But this attitude seemed to disturb Jesus. He had been in the household of Martha, Mary, and Lazarus frequently, and had no doubt revealed to them many more intimate things about Himself than were actually recorded in the Scriptures.

His next declaration was, "I *am* the resurrection, and *the life:* he that believeth in me, though he were dead, yet shall he live: And whosoever liveth and believeth in me shall never die. Believest thou this?" (John 11: 25, 26). This was most likely something He had been trying to communicate to Mary and her family before. He was grieved for them because of their unbelief; they were worrying about a dead Lazarus, when Lazarus's *real life* was standing right before them: Jesus Himself. His words to Martha could possibly have been put, "But *I am* Lazarus's life, the one and only life! How can you think that Lazarus's life is gone?"

This account of Lazarus's death continues, with Jesus encountering Mary and the other Jews, all weeping. It is then that the scripture records Jesus as being troubled, and weeping Himself. The Jews took His sadness as an indication of His grief over Lazarus's death. It was, however, more likely sadness over His friends' inability to realize all that He was, and all that He had in store for them. He had told them that He was *the* life; but rather than just say that, He called Lazarus out of the grave as an example of what He said, an example they could see and feel.

John, in describing Jesus, said, "In him was life [the life], and the life was the light of men" (John 1:4). Jesus Himself said, "I am the way, the truth, and the life" (John 14:6). He is the one Life, not just the best of many lives. There is but one Life. For us as Christians, there is but one Source for our existence and identity: Jesus Christ. Christ, the one, true Life, is all that is real or important. And, as Christians, we can know that our oneness in Him is all that is real or important.

You may be wondering just what is this "life of Christ" that we have? It is your sense of "I am" here, now. It is God's own Spirit and always has been. Yet we never notice that. We only notice we are conscious but not how. This sense of "I am" is the miracle above all miracles!

This relationship with God is a living, personal union. It is not simply book learning, not even knowledge of the Bible. The Pharisees knew and outwardly lived by the Old Testament principles, but to them Jesus said, "But woe unto you, scribes and Pharisees, hypocrites! For ye shut up the kingdom of heaven against men: for ye neither go in yourselves, nether suffer ye them that are entering to go in." (Matthew 23:13) This is just another indication that the kingdom of God is here and now.

Christianity is not a lifestyle, but a person – Jesus Christ. The Pharisees were trying to use the scriptures to improve their (false self) life rather than letting the Scriptures lead them to leave not *just* their life-style but also their total old self, and to depend on *the Life,* Jesus Christ, as their real.

One of the most important things we can discover about the Christian life is that it is *not* a process of adding correct attitudes, knowledge, images, etc., onto our false self, or even getting out all the bad attitudes and impulses; but simply leaving that whole false person behind, whether it is good or bad or "together" or not.

When we discover a wrong attitude in ourselves, such as pride, for instance, usually we will try to remove, change, bury, or cover up that attitude with its opposite, right attitude, humility. We think this is repenting, but actually when we get to the bottom of things, the pride is still there and the humility was really just a false attitude we added on as a cover-up. This actually hardens our heart because it is really a lie. It is just like the whitewash on the sepulcher that Jesus spoke of. The Pharisees used the Scriptures as a guide to proper attitudes and action to look right to God and other people. But the Scriptures say that it is necessary to drop the whole person, self, your mental self image, from consideration and rely on the already perfect person of Christ *the Life* (Matthew 16:24-26).

Much of what Jesus said to His disciples in the scriptures is so close to us and so simple and profound that we miss it at first. Many things we think we know, we find out later that we did not really *know* at all. There are still things, no doubt, which we have heard over and over again, but which have not really sunk in yet. The sentiment, "Once I was blind, but now I see," becomes our experience time and time again. "Come to *Me* so that you might have life," is a good example of this.

In this writer's case one of the things which I thought I saw and understood was "coming to Christ" or "knowing God" and having singleness of purpose toward Him. I had been told, I had heard sermons, and I had read Scriptures on the fact that our eye must be single upon God. The verse, "... seek ye first the kingdom of God, and his righteousness, and all these things shall be added unto you" (Matthew 6:33), seemed very significant to me.

I thought, "That is the secret! The way to get all those things I want is to seek Him first." So I followed this route for quite a while-although without realizing it, I wasn't really seeking God, I was thinking, "Okay, God, I will seek You because I want those *things* (happiness, peace, security, etc.). "It hadn't really occurred to me that God the Person was worth knowing just for Himself. And in *that* God was offering His very self, His spirit, to *replace* my own empty, devious, false and greedy one.

Often we hear sermons preached (by preachers who should know better) upon this very point: by seeking God, they say, we can have His storehouse of plenty opened upon us. Whom do we think we are fooling? Surely not God. It especially becomes a source of sermon material at stewardship time. The theme becomes, "If you give more, you will get more; the way to get things out of God is to give first, so that He may reward you." Another variation is: "He has given so much to you, the least you should do is give Him a little bit back."

I wanted that storehouse. I did not want to appear to be selfish, but people had told me, "God has everything, and has made it all available to you. Why miss out on your inheritance?" It was as though God *owed* me something. Therefore, I seemed justified in my demand for things and more things-both spiritual and material.

All those Scriptures are true about God's wealth and His desire to give. But for us and for those who twist these words, the truths can become perverted into ways of thinking that reason, "Here is a way that I can use God to get what I want."

This mistaken attitude is, unfortunately, very natural to adopt. We feel that we really do need these things, indeed have a right to them, and must find a way to get God to give them to us. This applies to spiritual virtues as well as material things. So we search for the right button to push to make God respond; we cast about for the right prayer, the right Scripture verse, the right attitude to get results.

We flock to the popular teachers to acquire spiritual maturity. But our intention is still simply to manipulate God to our own advantage. We play upon His "vanity" and "fears" to manipulate Him as we manipulate others. We do not give a thought to the fact that He is Yahweh, the self-existent One (Exodus 34:6), who has no vanity or fears as we fallen creatures do. We can and are invited to reason with God and make petitions to Him (*see* James 4:2, 3). However, we cannot manipulate Him. Sometimes we confuse the two.

How can it be possible that we would have to cajole, plead, or trick God into giving us the things that we want? Jesus encountered this attitude, and asked, "If ye then, being evil, know how to give good gifts to your children, how much more shall your Father which is in heaven give good things to them that ask him?" (Matthew 7:11).

God is not waiting for us to happen upon the right approach or mature prayer before He can bless us with His gifts. He is *always, always, always* giving us His very best. To doubt this is to doubt His very character.

This book is not intended to be about how to get *things out of God* and down to us, but rather, how we may be translated from down here up to Him and created in righteousness and true holiness (*see* Ephesians 4:24). When we are abiding with Him and in Him, we find we do not need to think about getting anything at all out of Him. His "best gift," indeed His one and only gift, is, simply and astonishingly, HIMSELF! If we are His sons, then *He* is ours. And we are *His*. And He is everything.

In the beginning of our relationship with God it is almost impossible to desire Him just for Himself. At first we usually are after what He has, not just who He is, and it is usually only because we haven't really had a good glimpse of His person. This is not to say that God can't and won't materially prosper us or give us favor among men, He may or may not. But the real kingdom of God is *far more* than those things. And I don't mean just a lot of good thoughts and esoteric sounding mumbo jumbo either. What we will find in the person God is much more real, much more sure and substantial, satisfying, and lasting than any of those things. Then we are free to have or to not have things.

An old saint once spoke of loving God solely for Himself, simply for who He is. That may strike us as very spiritual, but something which we may not really want to do: for many saints have suffered greatly, and we just do not want to suffer. On the contrary, we are often looking for an end to our suffering by getting the things we need from God.

Suffering, we know by experience, is not pleasant. The thought of having suffered for the Lord in the past is desirable; the thought of doing so in the present is not. We distinctly do not like the idea of suffering, and have to admit so. We are very familiar with our flesh. We have lived with it for many years and know that it does not like suffering.

Perhaps, we might think, suffering publicly and heroically for the Lord may be tolerable. But the type of suffering with which we are most familiar is that which results from our own sins. We are not usually persecuted for fearlessly preaching the Word, nor are we thrown in jail by the Pharisees for healing people on the Sabbath. We go hungry, not because of preaching the Word of God, but because of losing our temper with our boss and getting fired from our job.

This is very inglorious suffering, and we detest it. But God often uses it to show us how useless it is to desire things of the old self which is apart from our real life in Him. He uses circumstances to help us realize that it is the old "me" seeking Him only for what He can do for it. He does desire to give us good things, but not to the nature apart from Himself, for it will only take us farther from Him. He has given us Himself, for in the long run He is all that will ever truly do us good. This is for *our* good, not His "ego." Unless we know Him, we really don't know we have true life (John 17:3). And giving things and virtues to the old self only fastens us tighter to that self and we are less likely to abandon it for His real self. The realization of this is far more precious than the most enjoyable gift in the world.

The Truth

A passage in Hosea reads, "Then shall we know, if we follow on to *know* the Lord: his going forth is prepared as the morning; and he shall come unto us as the rain, as the latter and former rain unto the earth" (Hosea 6:3). This is most significant. If we follow on to *know* the Lord, we shall know. He will come to us like rain.

This kind of *knowing* is not just knowing *about* God. If we seek only doctrinal understanding, we head off into darkness. Wanting to know only intellectual things about God is a lust for knowledge; it is actually eating from the tree of the knowledge of good and evil!

A good education and sound Bible knowledge is necessary, but we often confuse knowledge with the knowledge of the truth. The Apostle Paul warned that in the last days there would be men who were "... Ever learning, and never able to come to the knowledge of the truth" (2 Timothy 3:7). If we are after knowledge in itself, we will find our search to be "... labor for that which satisfieth not" (Isaiah 55:2). The more we get of it, the hungrier we become. This is the knowledge of good and evil that is desired to make one wise; it traps us, and it kills us. *The common reason we want to understand and figure out something is so that we can master it and use it to its own advantage!*

We hear that the knowledge of the truth is good, and we think that this means we are supposed to gather a lot of knowledge about a lot of truths. But Jesus said, "I *am* ... the truth" (John 14:6). The truth is a Person. Knowing Him, in a relationship of union and love, is the only knowledge we need. "... Christ ... is made unto us wisdom, and righteousness, and sanctification, and redemption" (1 Corinthians 1:30). There is a desire to know God for ourselves from the viewpoint of ourselves. That is of the old carnal "me." But God desires us to know Him for Himself *from* the viewpoint of Himself. This is why we are created in Him. Let us go on to explore what He has provided for us so that we may enter into the experience of His love and being in liberty.

We read earlier of the idea we sometimes have of trying to get things out of God, of trying to determine what is His and what is ours. We discussed the way in which scriptures are used on God to try to force Him to give us things. In warning of this attitude, I do not mean to imply that God is unwilling to give us His plenty. He is the maker of the plenty; He provided the inheritance. He came down in a human body like ours, except that He was without sin, and sacrificed Himself so that we could receive our inheritance. He would, therefore, be the last one to keep it from us. And He certainly would be the last one to want us to use scripture to pry His gifts out of Him.

We sometimes picture God as some sort of slightly sadistic Father who says to His children, "I will give your supper to you when you use the right words and do a certain trick. I won't tell you what the right words are, but you may not have your food until you guess the right words and do the trick." Would we do this to our children? We might want them to learn to say, "Please," or something, but we would not make them go through gymnastics for the things they need.

We, even as fallen creatures, love our children and want to give to them. How much more, therefore, must God, our heavenly Father, who sent His Son to die for us, want to give us His gifts! He went to great lengths to bring us to Himself; He certainly is not going to make it hard for us now. If we are not enjoying what He has provided for us, then there must be something else wrong.

Usually that "something else" is the fact that we need to know which "us" God is referring to. We imagine our self to be the "me" we have created in our mind as an image of our self. This old "me" is of the old Adam creature which God has made void through the cross. That person is not known by God and therefore cannot know God and His kingdom. But if a sentient being hears and understands that Christ is its true self (not the "me" that he knows as his self), and that soul turns from the false life to count on Christ, he is then a new creature in

Christ. Since Christ and God are one, then also is the new creature one with God and His kingdom through Christ. So we see then that it is the "us" in Christ that is *already* receiving *His* plenty. The "us" in Christ will desire the things of and for Christ. The flesh "us" as self will desire the things of and for self. But we are no longer the fleshly "us" of self if we regard Christ as our true life-the truth-from God, for us. We don't have to "try" to be more Christ like, we just simply live joyfully and let God take care of behavior while we rest in Him.

But if we don't know this we will identify with the old self and we will be blind to what God is giving-Himself and His kingdom. Our eyes will be looking for things other than those He is giving because we want it for the *false* self (James 4:3). Our attitude then in coming to Him is, "What does He have that is worth something to me?" There is plenty: we are shown the heavens, the glory of God, salvation, healing, and so on. We come to Him because we (following after the false self) can use these things. And we get them, but we interpret them from the old self's point of view and once again we are looking for something other than what God is really giving.

We receive salvation, the Holy Spirit, perhaps healing; we feel, "Glory, Hallelujah!" But then we start having troubles. Perhaps we blame our problems on demons. We cast them out and rebuke the devil for messing up our good time. We go through all the correct motions, but wonder why we are not receiving the right things from God. We then line up Scriptures and say, "Okay, God, these are the things You have promised me, and here is a Scripture that proves it." And we try and make sure that everyone has been treated fairly, both God and ourselves-especially ourselves.

Try to envision a marriage that works on this basis. "Okay, wife, here is what you owe me in our marriage, and here is what I do for you." What kind of marriage would that be? It might work legally as a contract, but there would be no life in it, no love in it. That is not oneness. Christ frequently used-marriage as a type to show what our true relationship with Him is like.

But all too often our relationship with Him is as absurd as the marriage just described. We think in terms of what God owes us, and what we owe God. We try to divide things properly, so that we get what He owes us if we give Him what He asks from us.

We are always interested in the conditions. If we pray this way, God will do such and such. If we give our 10 percent, He will shake the money tree and pour out money upon us. We will get our blessings if we step out on a limb to prove to God that we trust Him. But then we often end up muttering bitterly, "God, I did my part; where were You?"

And we become angry with God, and go back to our Bible to restate the promise Scriptures, and on and on. This is the same bargaining relationship described earlier in the marriage situation. It is as though the husband said to his wife, "Here is my car; you may have this specified amount of my time in the evening. I did my part, now according to the contract I can demand something from you." And the wife would say to her husband, "All right, I will cook your meals in exchange for this and that."

A marriage is not intended to be this way. In a real marriage, the husband gives himself to his wife, and the wife gives herself to the husband, "... and the two shall become one flesh" (Genesis 2:24). And so is it between God and us. Is our inheritance healing? Is it all the blessings mentioned in the Bible? Does it come down to, "What does He owe me and what do I owe Him?" What *is* our inheritance? HE is our inheritance! We are no more two, but ONE in Christ. HE is our life, our silent awareness! How then can we divide things if we are one and He is our life? Only when we identify with the old "me" do we think in terms of two separate lives and begin to divide things and interests.

He belongs to us; we belong to Him. He Himself, not just what He has, is our inheritance. We leave the old "me" behind, as it was never really us or ours anyway because of our real life in Christ. We have all because we have Him, and all that really is, is Him and Him only. If anything is not Him it is not worth having; it is unreal and temporary. But all that is Him, we have already, because He gave Himself to us. HE IS THE KINGDOM!

3
Graven Images

"Thou shalt not bow down to any graven image"

Deuteronomy 5:7-9

The above quote is one of the Ten Commandments that God gave to His people, Israel. Upon hearing it, our thoughts immediately shift to other lands, other times: either to idolaters of old, or to natives of cultures very alien to our own. We envision tribes performing strange rites and sacrificing material goods, even human lives, to the carved images they have set up before themselves. These romanticized notions keep us from applying God's commandment to our own manner of living. None of us, we think, is foolish enough to bow down to hand-fashioned idols!

Let us, however, examine the nature of these idols which men have bowed down before to worship. Many times these images resembled men, or beasts, or some exotic combination of the features of both. Whatever their form, they were representative of part of God's creation, rather than God Himself. As Paul said, "... instead of worshiping the glorious, ever-living God, they took wood and stone and made idols for themselves, carving them to look like mere birds and animals and snakes and [mortal] men" (Romans 1:23 LB). "And so, since they did not see fit to acknowledge God *or* approve of Him *or* consider Him worth the knowing, God gave them over to a base *and* condemned mind to do things not proper *or* decent *but* loathsome" (Romans 1:28 AMPLIFIED).

We may feel that we do not behave so foolishly in present times, but we are wrong. Idol worship is just as widespread as ever, but now appears in perhaps subtler forms. I am not talking about such possessions as automobiles, televisions, etc., which many people call idols, but about something much more basic. We sacrifice our possessions, labors, and daily lives to a god just as false and grotesque as any carved statue: our totally imaginary self-image. Its very name implies that it is an idol.

This image is fashioned not in wood or stone, but in our mind and in the minds of others. It originates in the deepest, most basic, though unconscious, hunger of every sentient being: the need to be a real person. There is no bypassing that need. But, unfortunately, we secretly know ourselves to be nothing but a melting pot of things outside us.

Are You Living For The Wrong Self?

All that we think is truly us turns out to be bits and pieces of mannerisms and attitudes that we have copied from other people, books, movies, etc. We are like a stage set that has the appearance of something real but actually has no substance behind the facade. Within us, attitudes, ideas, and opinions have been added and removed over the years, like different furniture for different acts, and we say "this is me," but nothing really belongs. We are bare and empty, no matter how deep our feelings seem to be.

However, in our self-image, we will never admit to this. We try to gain a type of existence by living in the minds of others. We try to prove our reality by the evidence of the impressions we make on other people. Having them see our nothingness would never do; so we must build images for people to look at, images of the real person we would like to be, but cannot be. It is much like trying to make the stage believable.

If it works, and those around us are suitably convinced, then we establish our existence on the basis of their opinions of us. We even fool ourselves. But it is all an act, and we secretly know it. Our images are phony, and all that we define as our personality is utterly false. At best we are mere ghosts and shadows living only in imagination. "The heart is deceitful above all things, and incurably sick; who can know it?" (Jeremiah 17:9). The only real thing about it all is our bondage to it.

And under the phoniness is shame. If we ever consciously discover our true condition we are ashamed of our deceit, helplessness, and worthlessness. We are so constantly under condemnation that we are accustomed to it. But rather than openly admit to our state, we usually try even harder to hide behind our created images because we don't know what else to do about the situation. When Adam and Eve identified with their body and mind as themselves, they realized their nakedness and they tried to hide from God behind the bushes. We read the account of their lives, and marvel at their foolishness in trying to hide from God, yet somehow fail to see the very same attempts in our own lives.

We hide behind the way we dress, the way we act, the things we've accomplished. As it was with Adam and Eve, we secretly know that we cannot hide from God. But often our fellow men are deceived, so we continue. We rely upon the deceptions we have built in the minds of others, and thus feel that we inhabit a tolerable semblance of reality and have some self-worth.

Unfortunately, though, however satisfactory a god our self-image seems to be, whether it is a religious zealot or a free thinker, it is nevertheless an idol, and requires sacrifice. To it we sacrifice our own lives and the lives of those around us. We are horrified by tales of bizarre rituals in which children are sacrificed to graven images, but remain unmoved by the similar actions in our own lives.

We may not actually murder those around us, but we feed on them, manipulate them, subject them to pain and indignity, in order to please and protect our image. The easiest way to exalt our own image is to denigrate the image of someone else. Those nearest to us are the most likely to suffer attack.

Our self-image is like a petty god and very demanding. We continually scheme to bring others to worship and bow down before it. The great frustration and hurt we experience when others mistreat or ignore us arises because we feel they have not paid proper respect to our self-image we call "me." This holds true for the shy, retiring person as well as the outgoing egotist. Each feels the need to be seen a certain way.

A Self-Existent One

What is it exactly that we are calling the false self, a.k.a. "me" the ego, the self-image, the imaginary self, the illusory self, the flesh, the old nature, etc.? If we look within our self, we will find only the idea of self but not any actual self.

Just try to find one right now...

We have probably never looked for one before because we have always just assumed we were a self, an objective entity, a body/mind. But all we will ever find is a vague, ever changing image in the mind. We can even list specific attributes we have, but find no real self. Even the body cannot be counted as "me," for we could remove body parts, one at a time, yet never remove the part, "me." So the outcome is that absolutely all of our actions and concerns are based on taking care of, protecting and satisfying this vague mental imagination of what we think and feel is "me." However, when we find out all there is, is this ever changing mental self-image we are reluctant to believe it. After all, it *is* more than a bit frightening. But, at the same time it is a momentous and liberating discovery. The false self doesn't actually exist. It is only our imagination.

Original sin is simply thinking we are a separate self-existing entity apart from God. We think we are our body/mind. But don't worry, we will soon find out what God has done about this unsettling dilemma.

Such is the life lived apart from the reality of union in Christ. It is an existence based totally upon our own deception and the opinions of the people around us. Yahweh, one of the names for God in the Old Testament, means literally "the self-existent one" (Exodus 34:6). The serpent promised Eve that they would be "as gods." We try to be self-existent ones, but simply cannot. We try to exist in the minds of others, and for the minds of others. There is no reality in us; yet we continue along, making a feeble reality out of what we imagine others believe is true of us. If they can be made to believe, then it is easier to convince ourselves. However, we think we are being "individualistic."

That existence is, of course, extremely precarious. In relying upon what others believe of us, we become subject to restless fluctuation, for they are also relying upon our reaction to their self-image. Even if we are saying to ourselves, "Me? I don't care what other people think about me," we are just trying to build the image of someone who doesn't care what other people think about them. Self is self-conscious. Other people's whims and illusions do affect us, and that effect in turn affects them. All are in the same predicament, and on and on it goes.

In this manner our existence wavers daily, depending upon whom we meet and how they react to us. If they are favorably disposed toward us, we feel more solid. If they insult us or tear us down, we are frightened and angry. Our graven image has been desecrated. We show them. We lash back at the offender (or someone weaker) and his image for the disrespect paid to ours. Often it becomes necessary to lie, cheat, kill, and destroy for the sake of our own idols.

Can we see the fear, the slavery, and the hell of this kind of existence? Trying to prove and satisfy self is like trying to fill a bottomless pit. It always says, "Just a little more." But, no matter how much it is given, the void just seems to grow larger and deeper. Do we see how our old nature's images can trap us, can force us to dwell constantly in unreality and deceit? If Christ is not our life, we are forced to erect these images. If we do not choose the reality of Him, we must build a substitute identity in our mind and in the minds of others. We choose to maintain a monstrous delusion because we fear our own nothingness. It's not that we don't really exist. It is only that the person that we think we are doesn't exist-the "me." We do have a real existence-in Christ. God doesn't take the old image and remold it into one similar to Himself-He doesn't deify it or replace it with another imagination. There is only one life, Christ, and He is God. God IS, and He is *other* than what we could imagine. That is why the new life we count on is a *hidden* life "For ye are dead and your true life is hid with Christ in God (Colossians 3:3). Hope is counting on that which we know is, but have not yet openly seen. In other words, "The just shall live by faith" (Romans 1:7).

Do we see how shifting and changing the false self is? This was what Christ described in His parable of building a house on the sand or the rock (Matthew 7:24-27). If we live in the false imaginary self, feeding on the impressions of others, we are building on sand. Our lives will be fleeting, constantly shifting, unreal. But if we will rely on Jesus Christ to be our life, our existence is solid: unmovable, unchangeable throughout eternity, independent of outward appearance and actions. For He is the Rock upon which all reality is built. Self-images force us to label our situations, such as bad, fearful, dangerous, etc. Every negative attitude of self brings with it a negative emotion which turns us from God and keeps us prisoners. With Christ as our life we need not worry about how things affect us.

Ye Shall Be Free Indeed

When our life is based only in Him, we can disregard our old dependence upon our feelings and the feelings of others. Other people can no longer change us when they change their minds, for our life is the unchangeable One, Jesus. Suddenly we no longer need sacrifices for our graven images, for we no longer need those images. We need no longer use other people.

This frees us to love them at last, to, love them with Christ's love. “If the Son therefore shall make you free, ye shall be free indeed” (John 8:36). We no longer have to prove others wrong in order to make our own selves appear right; nor need we prove them weak to make us appear strong, or prove them stupid to make us appear wise, or prove them evil to make us appear kind.

No matter how we appear or act, we find we are still the same in Christ Jesus, for He does not change (Hebrews 13:8, James 1:17). Our reality and our righteousness are in heaven, far above all principalities, powers, and names that are named. In Him we are in heaven, and in Him we are free, even from our imaginary self.

"If ye continue in my word, then are ye my disciples indeed; and ye shall know the truth, and the truth shall make you free" (John 8:31, 32). Sometimes we have to see that we are in prison before we will be willing to leave it. When the world collapses around us, it is simply that God is tearing down the "decorations" which camouflage our cell, the false "me," so that we may plainly see the bars and stone walls. If we take sides with Him against our own idols, against our own imaginary self, we will know freedom. At this point we are probably not only amazed at the many facets of our own self-image, but also concerned with how we can be completely rid of it and how much pain will be involved. The truth that will smash those images is discussed in detail in chapter 5, The Romans 7 Syndrome. We will also find out how one of God's own acts has bound us to these images, but only for a time and only that we might see of what they are made. We will discover that the rope that binds us to these images is actually His own law- the Commandments. Until we see how we are free from the law through the body of Christ, it is sure that these images will continue to haunt us. But after that, the fear of injury to our petty idols will be replaced by the permanence of His reality and love. "Perfect love casteth out fear" (1

John 4:18). Because self is precariously balanced and mortal, it is full of fear. When we participate in self, we are trying to live in a lie. We know this deep down, and we fear discovery. We need to be somebody, and fear that we are not. But Christ is now our life. Our identity is in Him, and we do not need to be somebody. Because there is nothing left to harm, and no more need to prove ourselves, we now have nothing to fear.

Unlike us, God has no image to uphold. He is always spontaneously and naturally God, and what He does always shows perfectly what He is. This is hard for us to believe because we are so accustomed to living with the guile and deceit of a false self. We find it hard to conceive of anyone, even God, as absolutely innocent and guileless. The purpose of the Holy Scriptures is to reveal His nature and character, so that we can completely abandon ourselves to Him. His omnipotence and unchanging love show us that we can completely change our frame of reference from ourselves to Him. That is obeying the truth!

In having faith in Him and in learning to know Him, we will find that the images cease to be a part of our life. We will no longer have to "be" anything, because Christ "is" for us. Instead of a law to keep, "Thou shalt not bow down to any graven image," it becomes a fact that we can count on when Christ is our life.

4
The Exchanged Life

"I am crucified with Christ: nevertheless I live: yet not I but Christ liveth in me: and the life which I now live in the flesh I live by the faith of the Son of God, who loved me and gave himself for me."

Galatians 2:20

The Meaning Of "In Christ"

Let's suppose that we bought an expensive new rocking chair and brought it home, only to find out that the seat cushion did not match the rest of the house. Would we frantically begin to redecorate our whole house in order to match the chair? Or would it be simpler and more practical to exchange the cushion for one which harmonizes with the rest of the house? That seems like a ridiculous question. Of course we would exchange the cushion instead of redecorating the whole house. Yet when our own self does not harmonize with reality, we try the impossible task of changing all the people and things around us, even God, to match our own selfish desires. But Jesus had a better way. He simply exchanged His own divine nature for our false imaginary self. His nature is already in harmony with God and all the universe; His nature already loves and enjoys life and fellowship with God the Father. Herein is rest and peace. We don't have to frantically exchange jobs, husbands, wives, neighborhoods; instead we can discover that Jesus has already exchanged lives with us. In this chapter we will examine that exchange more deeply. We will discover that *in Christ* we already are all that we need to be and we already have all that we need to have.

God never promises anything that has not already been fixed, arranged, and done. We do not have to do anything to get God to back up His promises; what He promises is. All we need is to realize that, and rest on His solid faithfulness. We do not need to prove anything to God. He is the one who told Moses "I am *that* I am." (Exodus 3:14). He is Moses' own sense of "I am." We can forget ourselves, and rest on the fact that we are in Christ. Our very sense of "I am" is God's sense of "I am."

"We in Christ," and "Christ in us," are two very familiar phrases in the Scriptures. However, the understandings that Christ is in us, and that we are in Christ, are two different things. For some reason, either because of our natural tendencies or because of the way the Word is preached, we think that after "accepting" Christ, He is in us, but that is where we stop.

Rarely do we manage to go on to see our place "in Christ," and what that means to us. Our union with Christ tends to be one of those things we might agree with, but do not really understand at all. When the reality of it does get through to us, something incredible happens. The revelation of our place in Christ is indescribable and totally transforming. It affects us for the rest of our days.

To know the meaning of He in us and we in Him, it is necessary to go back to the cross. We find that none of our own works qualified us to be found in Christ. He did all the work on the cross; we simply were included with Him there by the Father. Remember when we came to salvation? We were not resting upon what we did, but upon what He did.

We will be talking about two important aspects of salvation: substitution and identification. Substitution is from the point of view of what Christ has done for us. Identification is from the point of view of our being included with Christ in what He has done, is doing, and will do.

Whether we understood all of this at the time of our salvation or not, we came to Christ and might have said something like, "I see that You have provided redemption for me. I am guilty of infraction of the law; I fall short of the glory of God; I am a sinner. Jesus, You came in my place and took the punishment I deserved, because I never could have survived it." We saw what Jesus had already accomplished, what had already happened, and we relied upon it. He was our substitute in punishment and death.

If Christ died as a substitute for us, for our redemption, then we are counted as dead. When Christ died, we all died too.

If one died for all, then all died (*see* 2 Corinthians 5:14). This is *identification;* we died with Him and in Him.

Three days later Christ rose again in newness of life. Just as He died as a substitute for us, so He also rose as a substitute for us. Because He rose and is living for us we can say that we are counted as being risen and now existing *in Christ.* This, too, is identification; each of us can say, "There is a new me, and I am found *in Christ.* The person I have always thought of as 'me' died in Christ; it no longer counts for me. Christ counts for me now." We now exist *in Him* and only in Him. *Any identity we might think we have in ourselves was ruled out by the cross. Christ is our new self. We have exchanged lives with Him.* Hosea 6:1, 2 is a perfect Old Testament illustration of our identification with Christ.

SUBSTITUTION – Christ died for me.

Christ rose again and lives *for* me.

Therefore:

IDENTIFICATION – I (the self I imagine myself to be) died in (with) Christ.

He rose again and I now live in Christ (Christ's own identity).

So we see now that He did not just provide for us halfway. We may think that He died only to relieve us of our sins by His blood, and to keep relieving us of them until we die, but His work goes even further than that. He also took care of the source of our sins -the sinner-us.

Watchman Nee related a good example of this in an illustration using prohibition. He said that taking care only of our past sins would be like outlawing whiskey and destroying all the whiskey bottles in the area, but leaving the whiskey factories untouched. All the whiskey would be gone for the moment, but the whiskey stills would still be producing, and in a short time whiskey would be found everywhere again.

So it would be with us. Our soul needs the cleansing of the blood of Christ, but it is our sin nature (self) that weakens and holds us in sin's power. Our sin nature is like the whiskey factory. It is a sin factory. God did not break all the "whiskey bottles" and leave the "stills" untouched. He destroyed the "stills," too. In our lives He did not stop at making provision for our sins, but He also took care of the person who loves sin. That happened when we died in Christ. Now He lives for us, as well as having died for us. He substituted for us, the Father identified us with Him. Our miraculous ability to be conscious and aware is God's own awareness. Our "I am" is God's "I am." But our thoughts are *not* his thoughts. (Isaiah 55:8)

Our identification with Christ means that we were counted by God as being included with Him, and in Him, when He died. We died, and thus are liberated from our false self, and the whole Adam race and liberated us from the law. The whole Adam race, or Adam creation, is built upon a lie, the lie that we are our body and mind. Through Christ we exited the whole dominion.

Entering into this new creation is a matter of recognizing Christ and His work and then counting on Him subjectively. We have no trouble believing that Christ died on the cross. The Bible also says that two thieves died with Him, and we do not argue that. We do not feel their deaths, nor are they around to testify of it, but apparently they did die. Nor do we feel Christ's death, but there is a good record of it, and we know Him and His Word to be truthful.

But the Bible says that we, too, died in Him. We may not feel as though we did, but neither did we feel that Christ or the thieves died. Self cannot understand how it can be dead, but still "aware;" but actually the "me" was always just an imaginary self-image existing in mind only, made up of a body image and imagination while our conscious awareness is God's own sense of "I am." This is a great miracle which proves our oneness with Him. We need only recognize it as so. By faith we understand (Hebrews 11:3). God's Word says that it happened, and it is just as surely a fact, no matter what self's feelings and experiences are. The Bible says we died, too.

"For if we have been planted together in the likeness of his death, we shall be also in the likeness of his resurrection: Knowing this, that our old man is crucified with him, that the body of sin might be destroyed, that henceforth we should not serve sin. For he that is dead is freed from sin. Now if we be dead with Christ, we believe that we shall also live with him: Knowing that Christ being raised from the dead dieth no more; death hath no more dominion over him."

Romans 6:5-9

To die in Christ means that we were separated from, or not counted as being one with, the imaginary Adam self which we have always known as "me." This "me" is the source of all problems.

That person, a mere mental image in the mind, is made null and void. The cross crossed it out; it X'd it out. The old phony creature "me" that we know as us, was made void two thousand years ago. It does not count. God does not fix up; He re-creates. His answer for man was not an improvement or repair job. He abolished the whole old creation (or creature), and re-created everything anew in Christ Jesus.

God does not take the old "me," fix it up, make it divine or Christ like, and put it in heaven. We were voided, and sent to destruction (*see* Romans 6:6). "When Christ died, all mankind died" (*see* 2 Corinthians 5:14 NEB). Nothing that we see of us, nothing of the old creation, counts at all. All was removed from consideration: our good as well as our bad, our bondage to the law as well as our bondage to sin. This is identification with Christ in His death.

In science fiction stories there are often speculations about time travel. One story is about a man who travels into the past and inadvertently kills his grandfather, then an infant. When he returns to his own time he finds, to his dismay that he never existed. There is no place for him anymore. There are even other people living in his house who have *always* lived there. If our grandfather had died when he was an infant, where would we be? We would have died in him; we would never have existed. And this is exactly our position in Christ.

The mind has just as hard a time trying to comprehend the death of the imaginary self as the time traveler had trying to comprehend his death. However, being imaginary, the false self never did really exist. But the penalty for sins is real. It didn't change the facts. "And the light shineth in darkness; and the darkness comprehended it not" (John 1:5). Meanwhile, all "new" sins will be attributed to the old creation which has passed away.

"But the natural man receiveth not the things of the Spirit of God: for they are foolishness unto him: neither can he know them, because they are spiritually discerned" (1 Corinthians 2:14). Now that doesn't mean that we won't ever understand anything, just the old "me." Christ our true life knows Himself and "[He] is made unto us wisdom" (1 Corinthians 1:30). "Through faith we understand" (Hebrews 11:3).

The *whole* identity of the Adam creature died in Christ. "For, behold, I create new heavens and a new earth: and the former shall not be remembered, nor come into mind" (Isaiah 65:17). This will not happen because our memory will be obliterated. We are simply going to come into the reality that already is. That is where we really exist.

Alive Unto God Through Jesus Christ

Up to now we have largely been concerned with the fact that we were included with Christ in His death and that, as a consequence, all mankind was voided and removed from consideration. The whole Adam creation was sent to destruction. Christ's death affected the whole universe, but it still is not all of Christ's work: we also were included with Him in His Resurrection.

We must clearly understand (by illumination of the Holy Spirit) and count on our death and removal in Christ before we can participate in the next part of Christ's work on the cross. We cannot partake of Christ's life without first partaking of His death. "For in that he died, he died unto sin once: but in that he liveth, he liveth unto God. Likewise reckon ye also yourselves to be dead indeed unto sin, but alive unto God through Jesus Christ our Lord" (Romans 6:10, II).

All that is now true of Christ, is also now counted by the Father as true of us. Paul explained, "If ye then be risen with Christ [we were included with Him when He rose!], seek those things which are above, where Christ sitteth on the right hand of God. Set your affection on things above, not on things on the earth. For ye are dead, and your life is hid (no wonder that we have not been able to find it) with Christ in God" (Colossians 3:1-3).

God is not trying to make things confusing for us. He simply wishes us to leave the earthly, imaginary "me" that we've always known and instead count on our life (identity) where it really is in Christ in heaven. This will be revealed to all creation on the last day, but even for now, when we turn our gaze upon Christ we will know that someone else is there with Him: ourselves. “When Christ, who is our life, shall appear, then shall ye also appear with him in glory” (Colossians 3:4). It is necessary to restate that God did *not* make the old “me” divine or Christ, or even real, but gave us a new self-the real life of the risen Christ. Christ is sharing Himself *as* us. That's what Holy Communion is all about.

Paul had other interesting things to say about our inclusion in Christ's Resurrection. He speaks of the resurrection power “... which He [God] wrought in Christ, when he raised him from the dead, and set him at his own right hand in the heavenly places, far above all principality, and power, and might, and dominion, and every name that is named, not only in this world, but also in that which is to come” (Ephesians 1:20, 21).

For many Christians the last statement's emphasis possibly could be changed to “not only in the age to come, but also in this age.” Our position in Christ in the heavenlies is not just for later, but for right now. Paul continues, saying that God “hath put all things under his feet, and gave him to be the head over all things to the church. Which is his body, the fullness of him that filleth all in all” (Ephesians 1:22, 23). Notice again the past tense.

It has already happened where reality is! A little later Paul says, “But God, who is rich in mercy, for his great love where with he loved us [it's His love for us that counts]. Even when we were dead in sins, hath made us alive (or quickened us) together with Christ, (by grace [or by His loving kindness and favor] ye are saved); And hath (past tense!) raised us up together, and made us sit together in heavenly places in Christ; That in the ages to come he might show the exceeding riches of his grace in his kindness toward us through Christ Jesus" (*see* Ephesians 2:4-7). "Who [God] hath delivered us from the power of darkness, and hath translated us into the kingdom of his dear Son" (Colossians 1:13). That is not only the most astounding but also the most important news a man can ever hear. Let's ponder it until we understand it!

It is quite possible to have heard all of this and still have it mean absolutely nothing to us. We may feel, "That's great. It is nice to find out that we are in heavenly places with Christ Jesus, but what does that have to do with things down here now? I have doctor bills, and people are bugging me, and I am sick and discouraged, and my best friend has turned out to be a slob, etc., etc."

The reason we may not experience the riches of life with Christ in the heavenlies right now is that we may believe it in theory, but in practice continue to look at and identify with *self* (the old "me") instead of Christ. Self was ruled out by the cross. What does our life in Christ have to do with what is happening to the old "me" below? We must see that those things that are all going wrong do not affect our *real* life, which is safe in Christ. When we realize that, heaven becomes now and here by faith.

Paul urged the people at Colossus, "If ye then be risen with Christ, seek those things which are above, not on things on the earth" (Colossians 3:1, 2). This was not a law. He was simply stating what *was:* we are risen and in heaven with Christ, and should think from that frame of reference.

He said in effect that *we* are there, and that we should consequently set our minds there, too. We are in heavenly places. "Heavenly places" is here now! "... it doth not yet appear what we shall be: but we know that, when he shall appear, we shall be like him; for we shall see him as he is" (1 John 3:2). We can discover Christ in heavenly places, for that is where we are.

We are in a place that is far above all principalities, powers, names, dominions, etc. We are positionally beyond the reach of anything evil (including demons and our old self); we are in the reach of God the Father. The Adam nature, deep in sin, is far removed from our true life. We are in touch with God. Remember, the other half of the phrase which begins, "... reckon ye also yourselves to be dead indeed unto sin ..." is "but alive unto God through Jesus Christ our Lord" (Romans 6:11).

Readers' Note: If some readers are still seeing all this as some sort of mind trick or willpower, they need not despair; it isn't either one, it's the power of God. Continue on, while seeking God prayerfully. As we proceed, somewhere along the path, almost imperceptibly, realization will quietly begin to grow. That little seed will never stop growing.

We are accustomed to living by the old self related understandings and feelings. We think that if we do not understand or experience something by our five senses first, then it must not be real. Recently this writer was trying to show this to a young man, who said to him, "I want something real." I asked him what he thought was real, and he said, "What I feel is real." He was mistaken, but his experience was a common one. Our emotions will tell us that something cannot be real unless we feel it, and if we feel it then we cannot deny it. Our feelings were originally meant to serve us, but when Adam fell, he became the slave of his feelings and to his own thoughts. Sin and sickness and problems, in fact all the things that are wrong with the Adam creation, are indeed there, but through Christ we have been removed from them. All things are put under His feet, whether we see it yet in time or not. Our position in Christ is separate from our old self's feelings and thoughts. It is possible to turn around and not require the feelings to follow. You are *not* your feelings or your thoughts.

In other words, we do not have to feel something is true and real before it is. Reality already is, whether or not we feel, perceive, or even believe it. Believing Bible facts, though, can bring us to experience what is already a fact, even though our feelings and thoughts might initially disagree.

In some religions the faithful are told that they can make things the way they want them by affirmation or believing. True Christian faith is not trying to make something the way you want it by believing or affirming; but a Christian believes because of what *already is true in Christ,* which is infinitely easier. The power of the mind in altering things and events may possibly have some basis in the old creation, as the old creature is the product of a lie and possibly more lies might be powerful enough to change the previous; but that is not the same power that Christ walked in. Christ's death and Resurrection was the method God used to translate us into the kingdom--not the will (power) of the flesh (John 1:12, 13). We participate in the new creation by knowing it first, then simply resting in it.

This old creature "me" is much like a downtown building that has been condemned. It is still standing in time, and still very much occupies that corner of downtown property as the old "me" still occupies our mind, but notice has gone out that it is condemned and soon to be torn down. It is counted out and made void.

All the people who once had offices there have already left, because they believed the CONDEMNED sign on the doorway. A few tramps may remain, but no one who plans to stay. So it is with our old "me:" the old Adam creature, self, has been condemned. God is simply waiting for the right time to openly tear it down in time and reveal the new creature and creation, which has been from eternity.

In eternity it already is, but we just haven't seen it completely in time yet. Jesus said, "Destroy this temple, and in three days I will raise it up" (John 2:19). It has been torn down and built up again. But we do not yet see that fully, because redemption will not be complete in time for all of us experientially until Christ openly comes again.

He is trying to show us what is solid and what is not, so that we will not be left without when the old creation openly comes down. There will be a lot of people who will have spent their whole life in the old "me" self, and denied their true life, Christ.

The Bible also talks of a group that will be saved, but as if they survived by fire (*see* 1 Corinthians 3:12-15). They will have been of the new, but will have almost always been abiding and participating in the old. When the old "me" is openly removed they will remain in Christ, but will feel as though everything is gone.

Because what they knew as themselves was of the old creature.

But for those who have been counting on and participating in the new creature, the only things to go will be the things of the old creature that have hampered their relationship with God through the deceit of sin. This is "believing on the Lord Jesus Christ;" trusting, relying upon, and adhering to, and counting on our life in the new. The Bible says that we are in Jesus, that He is in heavenly places, and we are with Him too, removed from all that is not Him.

The False Self And The Mind

Obviously, over the years of living for the imaginary self, the mind has acquired a lot of bad habits of thinking so the mind will, out of habit, tend to think along those old patterns and lead us into sinning. But, don't worry, it is not attributed to you. Continue in your scripture study and study this book and, over time, you will be transformed by the "renewing of the mind." (Romans 12:2) In the meantime, live joyfully in the Kingdom of God.

It must be clearly understood that the soul and the false self are not one and the same. We have observed earlier that at the fall of man the soul turned from God as its frame of reference, and, being nothing *in its self* (as it is created and sustained by God) it was unable to find another frame of reference (for God is reality), and was forced to fabricate a new frame of reference. The price was its own deception. This substitute frame of reference is what we now may call ego, self, "me," the empirical ego, sin nature, old nature, the flesh, the old man, etc. It is just a mental picture used as a substitute for God as the one life. It is a graven image. The false self is built upon the "sin principle" which is, as previously said, a self-concept incorporating the body and its senses with the faculties of the mind. The lie says that this concept is a true, complete, self-existent person in itself. But only God is the self-existent One. He is the only "I AM." We can only "be" in Him.

If we continue to look to this concept, the false self, for identity, it is held in sin and destruction. But God's desire is for us to look to and depend on Him for true identity or as the frame of reference and existence. This is now possible through the finished work of His Son Jesus Christ. We see then that the old "me" is the lie that turned us from our true life in God. It is a graven image designed to replace God in the mind that is trying to be as God or independent of Him.

How This Affects Daily Living

If something shakes us up we can ask, "Is Jesus shook?" If He isn't, then we can know that we aren't really shook either. Just the self image that doesn't count for us is shook. Whenever we sin, it is because we have simply, out of habit, turned from relying upon our true position in Christ and our oneness with Him. Martin Luther once said, "The moment I consider Christ and myself as two, I am gone." And Meister Eckhart, the 14th century mystic, said "if I am this or that I cannot be all things." As far as our life is concerned, it is really no longer Jesus and self, or Jesus and I and self. It is just Jesus. We are included in Him and nowhere else.

It's very hard to understand our oneness in Christ. This is because we normally think of our oneness in Christ by conceptualizing our self as a separate, objective entity. And, we also conceptualize Christ the same way, as a separate entity. However, we cannot conceptualize how our self and Christ can be one because we cannot picture or imagine how that would seem. Neither can we imagine what it could be like, or even how Christ can be one and at the same time many.

It is a little like watching a movie. On the screen is one light, but we see it on the screen as other people and things. Such is the Spirit of God. The reality is the light of the Spirit but the people and things are still made of the one light.

In the Bible, the word translated as "believe in" never meant just simple mental assent. The Amplified Bible translates it as "trust in, rely upon, and adhere to Christ."

He is sharing all of His very identity, all of His very life, with us. (He is *not* sharing Himself with the false self, but with the soul.) This is something beyond our wildest dreams! God loves us and wants our good so much that He is sharing all that He is with us, so that we might become one with Him even in experience. Through Christ's work on the cross we are so close to Him that there is no longer two of us, but one!

"I have been crucified with Christ-[in Him] I have shared His crucifixion; it is no longer I who live [the old creature], but Christ [the new creature], the Messiah, lives in me; and the life I [the new creature] now live in the body I live by faith-by adherence to and reliance on and [complete] trust-in the Son of God, Who loved me and gave Himself up for me."

Galatians 2:20 AMPLIFIED

Christ comes to us and shows Himself as *the* Way, *the* Truth, and *the* Life, or the I AM. The soul recognizes and responds to Him and in turning to Him it discovers true existence in Him, and gives up what it thought was its own self-existence. In seeing its real existence (Christ) it gives up its false existence (self).

We can put it another way by saying that the sentient being in trying to "be" in itself, ends up "not being" as it has no substance in itself (self is built on a mental picture, remember). But by giving up it's trying to "be" (its own false identity "me") and turning to Christ, it finds that in Christ it "is." By giving up its false existence it finds its true existence. For only in Christ does our soul find substance. This is exactly what Christ meant when He explained that He was the Bread of Life. He is the food and substance of our soul. Our physical body has its physical being of the food we eat, thus our soul has its true existence of the true existence of Christ. True existence is knowing God.

"He that loves his life shall lose it, but he that loses his life for my sake shall truly find it" (*see* Matthew 10:39), said Jesus. When John said, "He came unto His own and His own knew Him not" (*see* John 1:11), he was referring to those that do not recognize and acknowledge Christ as their life or the substance of (and for) their souls, but instead rely on the lie of their own self-existence. Scripture abounds with references to this fact.

Readers' Note: This writer hopes that all this is not too mystical sounding, but finds that in matters dealing with the cross and in defining the old and new creations, one runs into many seeming paradoxes and invariably ends up in this kind of language. While trying to explain the oneness of the new creation and that all things are summed up in Christ Jesus, the writer is forced into using dualisms such as you and He, and God and us, etc., in order to be at all intelligible. But the very act of doing so obscures that oneness. The writer is also aware that intricate theological language may impress a few scholars and intellectuals, but may mean nothing to God's sheep.

In marriage, both the man and woman leave their father and mother to become united. Jesus told us, in a sense, to expect to do the same (Luke 14:26). To participate in the new creation or creature, Christ, we must leave behind the old creature "me." This is *not* a long struggling process of beating self to death with Scripture. It happens spontaneously when we see that the old self was already made *void* on the cross. We don't have to crucify ourselves, we are already dead *in Christ.* "It is finished" (John 19:30). God doesn't pay any more attention to self-why should we? Only self is interested in how self is doing. Only self tries to "crucify our self' or "die to self." That is false asceticism and only establishes self-righteousness. We are not leaving self behind when we are always worrying and thinking about it. No matter what we do to or for self, God still considers it dead and it doesn't count for us. Nothing we do to or for it counts either. When these facts begin to sink in, things begin to happen. God has said to us, "Forget the old. It is nullified and counted out." The good we do in the old does not count; the bad we do in the old does not count. Temptation used to be terrible, because we were accustomed to looking at self. We always believed we were one with self, and self certainly did not enjoy undergoing temptation and denial.

However, because of the cross we are now one with Christ. Our soul has not been accustomed to looking to Christ to see how we really are. But now temptations and tribulations provide our soul with a perfect opportunity to become accustomed to looking to Christ. It simply becomes a matter of acknowledging Christ as our life and then we can enter into rest and live joyfully.

Whenever the Holy Spirit reminds us of where we truly are, our soul will say yes and rest. Those who say, "No, I have to take care of this or I will be hurt; I have to defend myself, die to self, crucify myself, get crucified, etc., etc." actually say no to reality as well as to the Holy Spirit.

We may often hear the admonition "we must die to self," but let us ask "who dies to self?" Christ? He is our true life. Does He have to die to self? We *do not* have to die to crucify, or kill our old self. You can't. It is just a habit of mind, and will subside. That's just *self* trying to crucify *self* or self-righteousness. We are already dead and crucified in Christ. Who then is left to die to anything? Christ already nullified us and made us void on the cross. We do not count for us anymore, no matter what we are like. Only Christ counts for us, and as us, now.

Likewise, denying yourself does not mean "deprive yourself," but to recognize what the old self is. It is not forcing yourself to do things you dislike and forcing yourself not to do things that you like. That is just self-suppressing self, and it consists of nothing but law and bondage. Denying yourself is very different; it involves simply seeing it is not you leaving self behind through the cross of Christ, and resting in Him in the heavens, regardless of circumstances.

The Holy Spirit is not trying to tell us, "Quit doing that evil thing, you slob, and do right." That is only the unregenerate conscience or imagination. The Holy Spirit will simply tell us, "Look where you really are. You are in Christ and a son of God! You are of heaven here, not of the world there." And when we begin to realize that, and say, "That's right! Praise God," then we begin to live in heaven and experience it. Walking in the Spirit is simply agreeing with the Holy Spirit when He shows us our true identity and position in Christ. Walking in the flesh is agreeing with the false self and denying the fact of our oneness with Christ through His work on the cross. Then begins the "renewing of the mind." (Romans 12:2) This allows the manifestation of the fruit of the spirit. (Galatians 5:22, 23) You will begin to develop more subtle instincts and spontaneously walk in the Spirit without even trying.

When we are encountered by temptation, we can indeed count it all joy because we are getting the chance to know Christ better. This should be encouraging, because it is an adventure, a privilege, and a joy. When our soul leaves the carnal world of "me" to find experientially what God has said is already true positionally, we find things in the heavenly places we never dreamed could be true.

And things also begin to change in the world around us. When we wanted so badly to appear holy we were was still looking at the sinner, and left God no room to live through our members. But when, in our thought and reliance, we leave the old creation to abide in the new, Christ our true life has a chance to be expressed. We then begin to experience that holiness which is Christ. His life (our true life) begins to well up inside us and work its way out.

If we clearly see these facts and believe and count on them, they will inevitably lead us to have the same objective as the Apostle Paul:

"That I may know him, and the power of his resurrection, and the fellowship of his sufferings, being made conformable unto his death; if by any means I might attain unto the resurrection of the dead."

Philippians 3:10, 11

Readers' Note: We have begun to see the marvelous thing that God has done to rescue us out of that wretched state of slavery to the false self and separation from Him and His kingdom and if you haven't already taken this important step into His kingdom, now would be an excellent time. It's always much better to see it for yourself rather than just hear about it from somebody else. If you are not sure whether you have taken it or not, or are not sure just how; then the following will be helpful.

Here is what to do:

Recognize that you are a prisoner of your false self and that you can only want and do what it wants. Also acknowledge that you are separated from the reality in the person and presence of God and that you could do nothing to be free from your old self by yourself.

You must understand, at least partially, how Christ has rescued you from the domination of sin and self by making it void through His own death, and that the Father has counted Christ Himself as your new life.

You can now *turn* from your old self (because you know that it doesn't count for you now and it is only an image of yourself in mind and never really existed) and begin to depend upon Christ and what He is and does to count for you. You are only going along with what's true since He is literally your *real* life, your conscious, awareness, your very sense of "I am."

The Holy Spirit will now begin to reveal more actively the person of Christ, the Father, and His kingdom to you. He will comfort you by reminding you of the person and work of Christ so that you can increasingly depend more upon Him as your true life. The Holy Spirit will make Christ and His love real to you and manifest Him in your daily manner of living.

Stop now and make sure you understand this; then we will go on.

5
THE ROMANS 7 SYNDROME

"For the law is the strength of sin"
1 Corinthians 15:56

"For if we have become incorporated with him in a death like his, we shall also be one with him in a resurrection like his. We know that the man we once were has been crucified with Christ, for the destruction of the sinful self, so that we may no longer be the slaves of sin, since a dead man is no longer answerable for his sin. But if we thus died with Christ, we believe that we shall also come to life with him. We know that Christ, once raised from the dead, is never to die again: he is no longer under the dominion of death. For in dying as he died, he died to sin, once for all, and in living as he lives, he lives to God. In the same way you must regard (reckon-KJV) yourselves as dead to sin and alive to God, in union with Christ Jesus."

Romans 6:5-11 NEB

The Last Ropes That Tie Us To The Old Nature

These verses just quoted from the sixth chapter of Romans are the backbone of the "exchanged life" as discussed in the fourth chapter of this book.

The realization that we are dead, indeed unto sin, but alive unto God through Jesus Christ (Romans 6:11) is usually dramatic for us, and we expect the results in our daily lives to be equally dramatic. Now, we think, we finally know how to please God and live a perfect life, and we promptly set out to do so. It seems so easy: we have Christ as our life and now have Him in us; therefore, the only thing left to do is to manifest Him. For we read right after those verses in Romans 6:5-11 these verses:

"So sin must no longer reign in your mortal body, exacting obedience to the body's desires. You must no longer put its several parts at sin's disposal, as implements for doing wrong. No: put yourselves at the disposal of God, as dead men raised to life; yield your bodies to him as implements for doing right; for sin shall no longer be your master, because you are no longer under law, but under the grace of God."

Romans 6:12-14 NEB

Soon, however, we begin to be faced by situations where we know that we are definitely not manifesting Christ. Thoughts of how we should be more loving, more patient, more free, less selfish, etc., begin to plague us. The vague, nagging feeling creeps in upon us that we should do something about this situation. But we do not really know what to do.

After all He has done for us, we feel, the least we could do would be to follow His will. We feel we should be totally and utterly surrendered to Him, if for no other reason than out of sheer gratitude. Somehow, though, we just cannot seem to keep this attitude. And the accusing thought that we are not even feeling properly grateful towards God makes us feel even guiltier.

The result is that we begin to withdraw into ourselves. Here God has given us this marvelous opportunity to let Christ live His life through us, but we keep disappointing Him. We begin to be introspective of ourselves and critical of others. It would seem that we have not really found this promised life of rest after all.

We thought that we would be able to stop sinning once we came to know Christ's presence in us, but it just does not seem to be working out that way. Also Romans 6:11 appears to be more about positive thinking than about the power of God. Even though we are grateful that our sins are forgiven, we would really like to stop all this sinning in the first place.

The above is a short summary of the symptoms of what we might call the "Romans 7 Syndrome," because the Apostle Paul experienced it and relates it to us in the seventh chapter of the Book of Romans. So do most, if not all, Christians experience this phenomenon when they begin to receive an illumination of the exchanged life. Seeing the possibilities for righteousness in the cross, but not its fullness, can make even it a bondage. Paul's own experience was like this:

"We know that the law is spiritual; but I am not: I am, unspiritual, the purchased slave of sin. I do not even acknowledge my own actions as mine, for what I do is not what I want to do, but what I detest. But if what I do is against my will, it means that I agree with the law and hold it to be admirable. But as things are, it is no longer I who perform the action, but sin that lodges in me. For I know that nothing good lodges in me-in my unspiritual nature, I mean-for though the will to do good is there, the deed is not. The good which I want to do, I fail to do; but What I do is the wrong which is against my will; and if what I do is against my will, clearly it is no longer I who am the agent, but sin that has its lodging in me. I discover this principle, then: that when I want to do the right, only the wrong is within my reach. In my inmost self I delight in the law of God, but I perceive that there is in my bodily members a different law, fighting against-the law that my reason approves and making me a prisoner under the law that is in my members, the law of sin. Miserable creature that I am, who is there to rescue me out of this body doomed to death? God alone, through Jesus Christ our Lord! Thanks be to God! In a word then, I myself, subject to God's law as a rational being, am yet, in my unspiritual nature, a slave to the law of sin."

Romans 7:14-25 NEB

We have seen earlier that God's provision for us is not a repair job on our old nature, but *total replacement* of it. He gives us not another Adam-type nature, but *His own* divine nature. There is no more two (you and Christ) but *one* (you *in* Christ). “But,” you say, “the problem is more with the old nature than the new one; it will not seem to get crucified and stay crucified. Even though Romans 6:6 says that it is already dead, and even though I reckon it dead and yield my members unto God, I still keep having trouble with it.”

You ask, “If I am really dead in Christ, then why am I still doing all this sinning?” Many, many times after starting out well, we get hopelessly trapped right here, and we cannot understand why. We may feel that Christ's work on the cross, explained in Romans 6, is not enough and that we will just have to compensate for it by having more laws and more self-control. But the trouble is not in the verses explained in Romans 6; it is only that we have not yet seen it in its fullness. Indeed, until we have seen it in its fullness, sin will try to twist the teachings to its own advantage.

We think we have seen how we are dead unto sin and alive unto God through Jesus Christ, but we really haven't seen it fully until we know also how we are dead to the *law* in Christ; for sin still tries to use the law to keep us in captivity. The law is a peculiar thing in this respect. For the very thing that we think we must have to keep us from sinning is at the same time the very reason why we are sinning! How can this be? The law is, after all, just and holy and cannot be ignored. But by trying harder to follow the law or by even trying to reckon self dead (Romans 6:11) so we won't sin, we find that the wants, needs, fears and habits created by living for the imaginary self only becomes more stimulated.

What a dilemma we are in. Doubled and redoubled efforts only make things worse. And just "letting go" is license and that also produces sin and condemnation. Even if we are strong willed and are able to hold ourselves in check (at least visibly) we only become self-righteous and still have to deal with our secret life in our heart. Shall we confess it or harden our hearts? Usually we do not even realize that we are doing this; we think we are trusting Christ in us, or at least trying to. We are, however, "trusting" Him to make our *old* nature "me" follow the law, which is something He never promised to do. By trying not to rely on self and choose Christ in order to keep from sinning, we inadvertently *do* rely on self because the one doing the *choosing* was self? But how could self *choose* if it's just imaginary? By actively choosing according to our wants we only stir up the habits created by the presence of the false self.

God has a completely unique answer for this dilemma of ours. It is neither law nor license, nor is it anything at all that *we must choose or do*. It will operate spontaneously within the soul as we come to see the fullness of the cross. The cross has the *power of itself* to liberate us completely from the law, sin, self and condemnation; and at the same time fulfill the requirements of the law in our daily manner of living. This secret answer of God was totally hidden from the entire universe until Christ's death and is still hidden to many even now. This unique answer of God's is called "the law of the Spirit of life in Christ Jesus" (Romans 8:2) and by the end of this chapter we will have discovered it ourselves.

This treadmill of sin and condemnation is also inevitable whenever we are preoccupied with what we think is Christ *in us* instead of being occupied with our true self, the sense of presence, the "I am." We are trying to fit Him into the old "me" (new wine in old wine skins). Now, the sense of Christ in us isn't just religious feelings, benevolent thoughts, or gushy emotions added to the old imagined identity pictured in our mind. We can tell this is happening when we find that our attention is always on ourselves and what *we* are producing and feeling, what we are getting, and whether we are maturing and changing and happy, etc. If we really are growing and maturing we will know it by the witness of our spirit with God's Spirit, we cry, "Abba, Father." When we are always concerned with our righteousness and feelings we can be sure we are under the law and, consequently, participating with the old false self. The result is more frustration and more failure.

But until we see how we are free from the *law* through death with Christ, we will not be able to forget ourselves and rest in Jesus. This is very subtle. Often we don't even realize that we are still preoccupied with our false self. That is precisely the problem. We think we are preoccupied with God and holiness, and admire ourselves for our aspirations for such high attainments.

We will *always* have trouble with sin and the law until we understand clearly who and what, indeed, was "crucified with Christ." We tend to think "me" or self is only the egotistical, selfish, lustful, etc., things *in us*. But the person named as self in the Bible was the *whole* identity of self or "me." Egotism, etc., is not self, only the *fruit* of the self; or we could also say the manifestation of the sin that controls the self. If it were possible to get rid of the egotistical, selfish, lustful, etc., impulses we would still have all of the carnal "me," and it would still be just as sin-controlled and just as bad. Neither circumcision nor uncircumcision availeth anything, but a *new creature* (Galatians 6:15).

So the old nature is not just the sin in us, but *us,* what we have always thought of as "me." Sin *totally* controls that nature "*me,*" and God must deal with sin, by dealing with that nature or identity that contains the sin. However, we are deceived into thinking that the cross is only for the "bad" part of us or the sinful impulses in us. We are glad to get rid of that. That is the part that made *us* look so bad, the part that *we* were ashamed of. But *we* happily hang on to the "good" part of self, and label that "Christ" or the soul or the new nature or the real me, etc. Since we read that our old sin nature was crucified on the cross, we expect that those bad traits (which actually come from bad habits engendered by the old self) will stop bothering us now, and that the good ones will gloriously shine out from us. Then everyone will know without a doubt that we are truly spiritual.

But it does not happen quite as we expected. Instead of the deep inner rest and Christ like countenance we anticipated, we find our life becoming a veritable battleground between what we think is self and what we think is Christ. We keep telling self it is dead, but that is not true reckoning (Romans 6:11). We may try to stamp out the bad part by "getting it crucified" through difficult situations; we try perhaps to cast it out, thinking it to be a demon. Next we resort to repressing it by willpower, or even attempting to understand it through psychology. We find we are running around trying to stamp out the manifestations of self while self "me" continues unchecked; in fact, it steps up its output. The more we fight it the better it works. By using self to fight self we only succeed in more strongly affirming self.

We watch ourselves constantly to make sure we are reckoning ourselves dead and constantly watching out so that we won't "step out in the false self" and sin; but, alas, all is to no avail. The promised victorious life simply does not materialize. In this battle between "Christ" and "self," etc., "Christ" somehow manages to be continually defeated. In disappointment we wonder, "Lord, I keep trusting You, and You keep letting me sin. People say that 'Jesus never fails,' but You seem to always be failing. Why? What is wrong?" Often we redouble our efforts, re-consecrate our life, make resolution upon resolution, pray fervently at the altar, and promise God that we will never fail Him again, and the very next thing we do is *sin!*

Sooner or later, if we really desire to please God, we will find ourselves in the middle of this, "the Romans 7 Syndrome." Many never experience anything beyond this, and they turn back. It may truly have all the appearances of a calamity, but because of it we do indeed have the opportunity to come to a fuller revelation of the finished work of the cross. It can bring us into walking in the Spirit: an experiential knowledge of God in liberty.

In believing we had to constantly choose between Christ and self in order to avoid sinning, we only stimulated the needs of self back into action and since sin controls self, we found that in trying to choose Christ self popped up and sin appeared also. The more we tried the worse it got.

What was happening was simply that sin, being opposed to righteousness, used the law's demands of righteousness to its own advantage. We believe that we must still keep our false self right by maintaining a standard of righteousness so we can be approved of God, etc. That sounds reasonable and since we know Christ is our life, we feel that now if we always choose Christ then we can avoid sinning and thus always be on good terms with God, approved of our self and our brothers and sisters.

The moment we accepted that premise, self sprang into action, as it is always motivated by fear of punishment and hope for reward. The very act of trying to *choose* Christ to avoid sin and procure God's esteem backfired. It is *only* the old self that fears punishment and needs reward. Thus it was self that did the "choosing." When self is activated, the bad habits in it then overpower us and rules once again.

How Christ Delivers Us

God rescues us from that predicament by showing us by the Holy Spirit that in Christ's death *both* the person "me," who lived by reward and punishment, and the law that obligated us to keep that self approved were slain. Neither pertain to us now because our only real identity is now in Christ.

This means that with no law there is no way of reward or punishment for self. The news that we are dead to the law and that Christ is our true self means that nothing is left for sin to use to activate the old self. There is: 1) nothing left to choose – we are already chosen in Christ; and 2) no one is left to have to choose – we are dead in Christ; and 3) there is no motive to choose because we are dead to the law through the body of Christ. *When the supposed will of the old self is not activated, sin cannot express itself* since sin lives in the concept of self and must use self as its vehicle. Instead we activate the habits of the old nature when we "choose."

"... No human being can be justified in the sight of God for having kept the law: law brings only the consciousness of sin."

Romans 3:20 NEB

The law was necessary to bring sin and self clearly out into the open. If it weren't for the law stimulating our old selves, how could we discover that we were such hopeless sinners, and that we were actually controlled continually and totally by the habits created through the imaginary self? Without the law to overtly stimulate the flesh (self), sin was too subtle and difficult to detect. But when the law clearly showed the standard necessary for true life and companionship with God, we were brought to our senses and discovered the law of sin working in us which had heretofore secretly controlled us all our lives. So with the law came realization that we couldn't follow it and, at the same time, condemnation.

It is plain then that without the law or standard we would not have seen the need to *completely abandon* our total concept of a self, both the "good" and "bad" parts (for we have found that we couldn't abandon just the sin in us as sin totally permeated and controlled us).

If we have been duly convicted of sin's total power over us ("O wretched man that I am!") (Romans 7:24), and if we really want to know God and true life we will see that we can't have it by trying to keep the law or standard. Nor can we have it by keeping our old self "... who shall deliver me from the body of this death?" (Romans 7:24). It is then that the Holy Spirit through the word can show us the answer.

In being identified with Christ in His death, God has completely ruled out or counted as dead *all* of our self or "me." Then we can be shown that since all of self is counted dead and void, then also is all of the law made dead and void as it was made for self to reveal our inability to act of ourselves. The penalty for transgression of the law is death; but we can now realize that its full purpose has now been fulfilled, first by revealing our slavery to sin; then the death sentence was fulfilled in Christ's sacrificial death, since God counted it as our death, also. Through Christ's Resurrection we were also counted as in Him meaning that His spirit, His sentience, His self (that is not sin-controlled) now is also our true, original self.

The new self in Christ, though, is beyond concept, just as Christ is beyond concept, thus we have no concept or mental picture of our new true self, only a name and the knowledge that it and Christ are mystically one. In Colossians 3:3, 4 we see that "... you died; and now your life lies hidden with Christ in God. When Christ, who is our life, is manifested, then you, too, will be manifested with him in glory" (NEB).

It is time for us to enter into the true grace of God in Christ. We are brought to abandon the false sin-controlled identity and depend upon Christ, upon whom and what He is. We are now reconciled unto God and can know His full unstinted love and the liberty of His very own life. The glorious result: we rest spontaneously in Christ and He employs our members for righteousness. How else can it be? He is our righteousness.

When we feel that we must choose Christ to be our life so that we will do the right and be approved, we are still acting as though we were bound to the care of the old dead self. We are still living on the plane of the knowledge of good and evil, blessing and calamity, just as we did before we were even Christians.

It is still the old way of life that centers on reward and punishment for the *old dead self.* Sin has deceived us if we still think we must choose Christ for blessing and saving our old selves; for haven't we just found out that our selves are dead in Christ and we have been recreated in Him? The work is finished. Since the old self is dead, we have no person or identity to be concerned about other than Christ. So in that sense we don't have to choose Christ to keep the old self righteous because we don't really have an actual old self and thus no actual volition and are free of any obligation to keep it righteous. Our new self, Christ doesn't need anyone to keep Him righteous. The soul can then rest. "Ye have not chosen me, but I have chosen you ..." (John 15:16). When some who might not be aware of this priceless privilege find out that we really didn't and can't make a "decision for Christ," or choose Christ, but that God already did all the choosing and translated us to heavenly places without even asking our permission, they might be tempted to ask, "What about my own will in this?" That doesn't mean that we can really have the false self back though, just as the Israelites couldn't go back to Egypt and instead died in the desert between the two (Hebrews 3-5). The land was theirs, but they entered not in because of unbelief.

We are incorporated in Christ forever and that is not altered by the wishy-washiness of fear of punishment and hope for reward of self. Only what Christ *is* and *does* can ever count for us now. Even if our mind is still relating to the dead self, the fact is that we are still *in Christ* and counted so by Christ and the Father. We often revert to thinking that the person we once knew as us still counts for us and feel that we must always remember to "rest it in Christ" or we will sin. But the fact is we are dead (made void) and are not required to worry about a dead man's righteousness.

So we find that if we forget and think once again in terms of the old self it has no meaning, for our real self is in Christ and He stays pure and He never thinks in terms of our old self. When we sin, we may still suffer the worldly consequences but it is not attributed to us because we are dead to the law.

We are dead and the law or standard of righteousness only pertains to the living. If we are counted as dead through Christ by God, how then can God at the same time regard us as transgressing His law? He can't regard us as both dead and transgressing at the same time. And He doesn't. That is precisely why Christ died. When we died in Him the requirements went with us to death. The choices and actions of the dead are void. Since Christ is living and is our true life then only His choice, feelings, and actions can be counted for us. The power of the cross is in the fact that it removes all choices between blessing and calamity for ourselves and gives the soul only Christ and blessing. “In the same way you must regard (reckon, KJV) yourselves as dead to sin and alive to God, in union with Christ Jesus” (Romans 6:11 NEB).

Since the choice and thought, etc., of the dead can't count, then reckoning can't be choosing Christ over self. Reckoning can only be an acknowledgement of what *already is-Christ* our life. Real faith is resting in that fact, not trying to always choose Christ, for as we have seen, that only activates the old imaginary self and all the habits and desires linked to that self and sin breaks out again. We can't and don't have to choose Christ-He has already chosen us. That leaves no way for sin to activate self by making us choose between blessing and, calamity. When word of the finished work of Christ reached us, we hadn't chosen Him, had we? The work and choosing was done by Christ; not because we loved Him, but because He loved us. Just as we don't believe in order to make something true, but believe because we know it already is true, likewise we don't turn to Christ to get God and His kingdom, we turn to Christ because we are informed that we already *have* God because we are in Christ, and we believe the report. Christ said, “My sheep hear my voice ..." (John 10:27). Beyond that the reason why one soul will respond to Christ and another will not is a mystery that only God can clearly see.

We are simply *notified* of the good news of victory in our behalf. "...faith cometh by hearing, and hearing by the word of God" (Romans 10:17). Faith, joy in the Lord, rest, and relief can be the only response to such news. Enter into rest when you stop trying and just let you life be lived by Christ. For that is what is happening right now!

Now, after all that, what makes us think that the false piety of a dead man can do anything to alter, for better or worse, our true life, Christ? What we choose or don't choose isn't the question now, it was all settled and over two thousand years ago. The law doesn't pertain to us anymore because we are dead. Our spontaneous response is to forget the dead man and what it reaps and begin to enjoy God and His kingdom forever through Christ.

This death in Christ means, simply enough, that the imagined person we think of as us was ruled out *completely!* There is nobody left apart from Christ to get spiritual, nobody left to turn anybody's life over to God. Nobody to put anything on the altar of sacrifice. Nobody for God to work with, to stop sinning, to make mature or process! Nobody to fall under God's law-because we died! Who do we think died? Who doesn't count anymore? *We* died, the person we once knew as us and called “me.” *All* of us.

Through resting in Christ, God will renew our minds to think from His point of view in eternity. This will stabilize our emotions and liberate us to follow Him in love, but that only appears as we discover that it is *already* accomplished in Christ. We can only glory in the cross. Our Christian walk is a discovery of what already exists in the eternal kingdom, not a grueling self-improvement course. Truly we can say as Christ did, “It is finished” (John 19:30). Now let's live joyfully and explore it!

“He made Him, who knew no sin; *to be sin* for us, that we might become the righteousness of God *in Him”* (2 Corinthians 5:21). Christ took our false identity upon Himself. That's what was behind His agony in the garden, the shame and separation from the Father during His Crucifixion. That's why He was counted among the transgressors. The reason for His seeming bewilderment and confusion was us. He did *that* for *us*. That kind of love is heartrending. “Oh precious Jesus, I had no idea You went *that* far. I am devastated, astounded, and awestruck. I am brought to fall on my face before that kind of love and sacrifice. I have taken Your love so lightly.”

"... one man (Christ) died for all, and therefore all mankind has died" (2 Corinthians 5:14 NEB). Period. How can it be any plainer? Christ took the whole race of Adam to death with Him on the cross. We have thus been made void and removed from consideration.

That Romans 7 struggle was only the self habituated mind considering and worrying about self. Consequently, because of the cross, we can neither be condemned for our sins nor justified by our good works. What can we do for a dead man? Otherwise, just live joyfully.

Instead of trying to impress God with what we are, we rest in what He already is. We don't try to stay in Christ. We know we already are in Him and always will be no matter how often we forget. Our true life in Christ doesn't forget.

That is true reckoning. That kind of reckoning has no fear of "stepping out in the flesh" or identifying with self, etc. The person who would step out in the flesh is the flesh, it worries about that kind of thing, but it is considered dead and doesn't count for us and we don't have to try to keep it looking good. God only counts what Christ is and does as ours. When the we rest in that simple fact we are *reckoning* (Romans 6:11).

Is this license then; is it lawlessness? Wouldn't self run rampant with no law to restrain it? We only need a law when there is a transgressor, and if we are dead where is the transgressor?

We are free from the law because we are "crucified with Christ, for the destruction of the sinful self, so that we may no longer be the slaves of sin, since a dead man is no longer answerable for his sin" (Romans 6:6,7 NEB). And since we rose again with Christ a new creature, identified with Christ instead of the sinful self so that we could live unto God, how could we and why would we go back to the dead, sinful, self that we were set free from-who is not even our real life? If the self is counted dead then its lusts and desires are not ours either.

We can't reasonably lend our bodies to the rule of sin, but if we should sin (and we will only sin when we are concerned with the old self and the habits it has engendered), we, being actually in Christ, are not held accountable since we are considered dead in Christ. Only what our true life, Christ, does counts for us. It is easy then to confess our sin in the body (for why hide it if it is not counted), and the blood of Jesus Christ will keep the soul cleansed.

At least three times in the New Testament the statement "the just shall live by faith" (Romans 1:17; Galatians3:11; Hebrews 10:38) is made, which is indicative of its importance to us. Paul takes this even further to say, "...whatever is not of faith is sin" (Romans 14:23). When faith is this easy, where is fear of sin and condemnation? Christ is even the Author and Finisher of our faith.

"We aren't saved from sin's grasp by knowing the commandments of God, because we can't and don't keep them. But God put into effect a different plan to save us. He sent his own Son in a human body like ours – except that ours are sinful-and destroyed sin's control over us by giving himself as a sacrifice for our sins."

Romans 8:3 LB

Once we see that the cross effectively dealt with all of our old identity and are convinced there is no one to live for but Christ because there is nothing left of the old us to be counted, either by us or God, then we also find that there is also nothing of us left to apply the law to. Actually there never was. The old nature was a self-image made of only thoughts, memory and imagination! Nor does sin have us in its grasp any longer. It can't express itself in our members. "So you, my friends, have died to the law by becoming identified with the body of Christ, and accordingly you have found another husband in him who rose from the dead, so that we may bear fruit for God" (Romans 7:4 NEB).

The verse just quoted is in fact the conclusion of the Apostle Paul's own excellent illustration of our freedom from the law and consequently sin's power over us.

He illustrates our freedom from the law like this:

"For the woman (the soul) which hath an husband (the false self 'me') is bound by the law to her husband so long as he liveth; but if the husband be dead, she is loosed from the law of (or obligation to) her husband. So then if, while her husband liveth, she be married to another man, she shall be called an adulteress; but if her husband be dead, she is free from that law; so that she is no adulteress, though she be married to another man. Wherefore, my brethren, ye also are become dead to the law (obligation to establish the righteousness of and cater to the desires of the false identity 'me,' because that identity is counted as dead) by the body of Christ, that ye should be married to another (your true identity in Christ), even to him who is raised from the dead, that we should bring forth fruit unto God. For when we were in the flesh (the old false 'me'), the motions of sins, which were by the law, did work in our members to bring forth fruit unto death. But now we are delivered from the law, that being dead wherein we were held; that we should serve in newness of spirit, and not in the oldness of the letter."

Romans 7:2-6

We now live in God, of God, and to God; we issue from God. We are the children of God. We are counted in with Him as one (2 Corinthians 5:17). We are in Christ, and Christ is in heaven on the right hand of the Father (Ephesians 1:20; 2:6).

Our true source of life and frame of reference is now Christ, not our thoughts, feelings, and image from the false concept of self; nor the laws and wrath of God that pertain to it. The old "me" is not considered Christ, of course, our real identity is counted to be the new one hidden in Christ.

When we talk about Christ being our frame of reference, it does not mean that we look from the old dead self to Christ, then to everything else; but it means that we look from Him, our true self, to the Father and everything else. We don't look *to* Christ, we look *from* Christ!

Christ's own identity, His holiness, righteousness, peace, joy, favor of the Father, etc., in fact all that He is, is now put to our account. The results: "There is therefore now no condemnation to them which are in Christ Jesus" (Romans 8:1).

God's Purpose In Giving Us Jesus

When we cease being concerned about what we are becoming, and concentrate on Him who is coming, then our becoming will be coming!

The whole purpose of seeing that we are in Christ is so that we can *withdraw our concern from self and put it on Christ.* This happens spontaneously when we realize the full work of Christ on the cross, which includes freedom from any obligation to take care of the old imaginary self. Our true life is hidden with Christ in God. It is then that we enter into the true rest and fellowship of God. Let your life be lived by the Spirit of God!

"Since you became alive again, so to speak, when Christ arose from the dead, now set your sights on the rich treasures and joys of heaven where he sits beside God in the place of honor and power. Let heaven fill your thoughts; don't spend your time worrying about things down here. You should have as little desire for this world as a dead person does. Your real life is in heaven with Christ and God."

Colossians 3:1-3 LB

"If ye then be risen with Christ, seek those things which are above, where Christ sitteth on the right hand of God. Set your affection on things above, not on things on the earth. For ye are dead, and your life is hid with Christ in God."

Colossians 3:1-3

The Law Of The Spirit Of Life In Christ Jesus

When our soul rests in Christ (by seeing that it's already there), counting on Him to be our true self, we are *abiding* in Him. Then He, by the Holy Spirit, spontaneously abides in our bodies which are in the world. What was already true in eternity is now fulfilled in time as we depend upon it. We are then sealed by the

Holy Spirit. Isn't that beautiful? Then we see the *real* fruit of the Spirit. Notice the order of John 15:4, where Jesus says, "Abide in me, and I in you." The soul abides in Him; then He can live His life, which is our real life, through us. (Remember that the new life of the soul is in Christ, not the old "me.")

The Holy Spirit is to reveal to the soul and bring to this body the person of Christ. Now we can live by Christ, that is, by His own life that works out through us *by His own instincts* (Galatians 2:20; Romans 8:3; John 16:13-15). All this happens when the soul hears what He accomplished for us and believes on Him as its true life and enters into rest. "... That the righteousness of the law might be fulfilled in us, who walk not after the flesh ('me'), but after the Spirit (Christ the real life)" (Romans 8:4). It is important to realize that Christ's life will come forth by *His own* instincts. Nor do we try to imagine what Christ would do and copy it. The old "me" cannot live a life like Christ, or even try to be like Him by receiving more of His power.

But we can now *live* in our bodies in and by the true person of Christ rather than in the imaginary person of self (or "me").

Note: Let us pause here for a word of admonition and comfort to the reader. It is feared that even in spite of this detailed explanation, that some, because of this writer's own limitations or through the deceitfulness of sin, will twist this picture of God's precious grace into a form of license for the false self, passivity, self-deification, or legalism. Those who do so will do it to their own frustration.

The new life in Christ is not to be confused with things like the "Christ" or higher self in every man that only has to be discovered and brought out by positive thinking, etc. There is only one true Christ and only through faith in His work do we become partakers of His divine nature. He is other than our apparent self. Anything other than that will lead the believer into deeper bondage to sin and self. True fruit of the Spirit (Galatians 5:22, 23) will be the evidence of a true faith (God Himself is the purpose). Also, our spirit will bear witness with God's Spirit. "whereby we cry, 'Abba, Father!'" (Romans 8:15)

This writer must count on the fact that God's sheep will hear His voice and all that are His will come to Him (John 6:37). These things are hard to understand at first. We all will fall into temporary confusions and sin will temporarily succeed in controlling our members; it is to be expected and one should not panic when it happens. Remember that we have believed the good news that we are considered dead in Christ, so our sins in the body are not counted to us. Only what Christ, our true life, does counts for us. We must just acknowledge it to God and He is faithful and just to forgive us our sins, and to cleanse us from all unrighteousness" (1 John 1:9). "If we believe not, yet he abideth faithful: He cannot deny himself' (2 Timothy 2:13). Let us also remember that the Bible is still our only infallible guide and unless our understanding meshes with the total Bible, there is still room for more discovery of His grace. This is an adventure, not a forced march, and should be entered into with zest and an enthusiasm for exploring the kingdom that we have already been given. We are not after our own perfection, we are discovering God, the perfect One.

The old way of living in the false "me" was either by legalism or license, or a combination of both, which only lead to bondage and death. But God in His mercy has given us a new, *spontaneous* way to live. This is called living by the law of liberty, or the law of the Spirit of life in Christ Jesus (James 1:25; Romans 8:2).

This law is higher and stronger than the law of sin and death, and supersedes it. Earlier we found it to be a law that, whenever we try to do good, evil is the result. Now we see a higher law in operation that whenever we regard ourselves as "in Christ," good is the result. This happens because Christ's life (our true life) is free to operate through our bodies and mind, and His life is free from the control of sin. Christ's life is not a foreign life, but the life we were intended to have. The old "me" is the foreign life, even if it was more familiar – it was only familiar to itself. Christ is the true Shepherd, "me" is the false shepherd.

Just as the self-life spontaneously and effortlessly sinned, so Christ's life spontaneously and effortlessly follows the divine will of our Father. Our soul will know His life more and more as it becomes accustomed to disregarding self, which we once thought of as "me," and looking to Him, whom we know now is our true life. Since our real life has always been in Christ, the soul need only rest there. Our frame of reference will shift from self to Christ. Trials then are able to be used to strengthen this habit, because with each trial we have the opportunity to be reminded of Christ by the Holy Spirit and live unto Him, thus forming a new habit of the soul.

Before we knew Christ, we were accustomed to looking at our self-image and the body/mind for our identity. But the self, controlled by self-centered habits, led us invariably into death. Now, thanks be to God, we have heard and believe that we are not one with self, but one with Christ. By the promptings of the Holy Spirit, we recognize that it is in Him and look to Him for our identity. The Holy Spirit will remind us that only what Christ is and does counts for us now, and we will be led invariably into life. Indeed, He is Life itself.

Our knowledge of God and conduct in the world is completely dependent upon this kind of relationship with Christ. Fulfilling God's laws and doing good works are always a *result,* never a prerequisite, of resting in Him. "Walking in the Spirit" happens when we agree with the Holy Spirit that Christ is our true life, and rest in Him in that knowledge. First we must know our oneness with God. Holy living in this world will then naturally "be added unto you."

6

Walking in the Spirit

"In Him was life and the life is the light of men."

John 1:4

The Life Of Faith Or How Peter Walked On Water

Living by faith is looking to and depending on Christ, rather than self's thoughts and feelings and outward conditions, to see our true condition. Peter, walking on the water, is a good illustration of this life of faith (Matthew 14:29). The stormy water represents our thoughts, feelings and circumstances. We know Christ as our new life, indeed the one and only true life, just as Peter did.

As long as Peter looked to Christ, he was experiencing his oneness with Him. In this oneness both of them walked on the water, even though the storm was still going on and still visible in Peter's peripheral vision. Just as the storm continued to rage, so will our thoughts, feelings and circumstances be snapping at us as we look to Christ.

Peter did not continue as he should have. “Peter stepped down from the boat, and walked over the water towards Jesus. But when he saw the strength of the gale he was seized with fear; and beginning to sink, he cried, 'Save me, Lord'” (Matthew 14:29, 30 NEB). When Peter saw the fierceness of the storm he changed his frame of reference from his true life, Christ, to his false life, Peter. At that moment he ceased to participate in his true life, Christ, who was walking on the water, and began instead to participate in his old life that always sinks. (Note, though, that Christ caught him anyway and he did not drown.) Even though his faith had fled, Christ was *still* his real life. Even though Peter wavered, Jesus didn't and Jesus held him up.

This is a good place to point out that walking in the Spirit is not following the instructions of some inner voice, as many people think. That inner voice is usually a combination of imagination and conscience, although it really can sound spiritual. It is admittedly better than no conscience at all, but that is not really walking in the Spirit. If we couldn't even follow the Ten Commandments, what makes us think we can now obey a multitude of commands all day long? If we are able, then it's probably just our flesh directing our flesh. Walking in the Spirit is a much more spontaneous thing if you even think about it at the time.

When we, by the Holy Spirit, look with our soul unto Christ and fully depend on Him as our true self, our experience spontaneously lines up with Him, for He is the Truth. The waves keep pounding, but do not affect us experientially. That is walking in the Spirit! It happens when we are not thinking about it. However, if we look away from Jesus, who is our life, and look at the waves, then we experience the weakness and hang-ups of self, and inevitably succumb to temptation and go down in what appears to us as defeat. We can't drown as we are always in Him and He holds us, but we really do not have to participate in any sinking. We can continue to rest in Jesus, no matter how high or threatening the waves may be, or how easily our old, imaginary "me" sinks. This is not positive thinking nor a way to close our eyes to our problems: it is a way to detach our identification from self, the power of sin, and temptation and walk in the reality and power of God on top of those problems, rather than flounder in them. Walking in the Spirit is actually the easiest and most natural way to live, because it is the way we were created and intended to live!

Peter walked to Jesus in order to be with Him, not just in order to perform the trick of walking on water. He could step out of the boat to go to Jesus because he knew that Jesus was his real life (identity), and that he was *already* walking on the water *in Him*. That's what faith is. Isn't that simple? It starts with Jesus and ends with

Jesus. All we need to know is who and what He is the – Way, the Truth, the Life. We cannot walk in the Spirit and overcome simply for the purpose of *that in itself.* Walking in the Spirit is the spontaneous result of our understanding that we are in Him and He is our true life. And that belief comes not from wanting to *use* Him for self, but from wanting to *know* Him. He bids us to come to Him, and it is then more than ever that we know our oneness with Him and participate in the wonders of His person.

The Bible says that Peter stepped out on the water *to* go *to Jesus.* That can be our only motive, also. Then we know as Peter knew that because He *is* our life and since He is walking in the Spirit, then we must *already* be doing it also *in Him.* He bids us come, and we step out. If our belief falters, He still has us and even though we sink-He doesn't sink. And He has a hold of us. "If we believe not, yet he abideth faithful; he cannot deny himself" (2 Timothy 2:13).

Let us see how this works in daily life: Because we are counted as in Him by the Father, then whatever He does we are doing also *in Him.* If our faith or understanding and experience falters, we are still safe for He holds us. "... though fools, [we] shall not err therein" (Isaiah 35:8). In resting in our incorporation with Him, we walk over temptations, problems, and fears simply because that's what Jesus does, and we stay free of the controlling power of sin. When we hear the news that we are in Him, knowing Him becomes our spontaneous objective. Our daily walk is simply one of the results.

At the point of our salvation, we did not *do* anything: We simply relied on the fact that we were counted in Him when He took our guilt and punishment and overcame sin and death, but as we have learned, our salvation did not stop there. Just as we were in Him in death, so also are we in Him in resurrection life. As surely as the Father counts our sins as paid for because Christ died for us, so does He count us as literally being with Him in heaven because Christ literally *is* our life. Christ is in heaven, and therefore we are, too. "Even when we were dead in sins, He hath quickened us together with Christ, (by grace ye are saved) And hath ... made us sit together in heavenly places in Christ Jesus" (Ephesians, 2:5, 6).

He became the sinner for us, and also becomes the righteous one for us. "For he hath made him to be sin for us, who knew no sin; that we might be made the righteousness of God in him," (2 Corinthians 5:21). We can stop looking at what our false self is doing and feeling. Because of Christ, our concerns and emotions from the viewpoint of the false "me" do not count anymore. We can participate in the body in anything that our real life (Christ) is doing. Since He is our real life, we must be already doing it. When our frame of reference is the truth (Christ), then in the body we participate in the truth. When our frame of reference is a lie (self), then in the body we participate in that lie.

The righteousness of God is not just for our own peace, but for our *fellowship with God the Father and His Son Jesus Christ.* And that means more than just talking to Him; it means participating in Him. If we are in fellowship with God, our actions will spontaneously reflect Him without our trying. Just as Peter knew he was *in Christ* and participated with Him and walked on the water the same way Christ did, so will we do as Christ does when we discover that incredible truth that He is our true self. If we are busy trying to make our *self* improve, our attention and fellowship will be with our *self,* and our bodily actions will spontaneously reflect the imaginary *self,* even though the truth is that we are in Christ.

Now that we see that the imaginary self no longer counts for us, and cannot possibly be of any benefit to us, can we not leave it? "If anyone wishes to be a follower of mine, he must leave self behind; day after day he must take up his cross, and come with me" (Luke 9:23 NEB).

We will always be able to tell when we are trying to put down the "bad" and force out the "good," because we will invariably be keeping all our attention on our *own* fruit. Our concern will not be with Christ (the truth), but with our self (the lie). Jesus, however, commands us not to abide in the fruit, but to abide in the vine, which is Himself (John 15). Do not attempt to attribute Christ-like qualities to your old false self (the one you once imagined was yourself) and call that your new self. It may flatter the ego, but will not bring you to God and true liberty.

When the branch is abiding, or reposing in one's new life, the person and identity of Christ, it spontaneously produces fruit. The fruit is of the vine, not of the branch. To abide in Christ simply means to stay where we are *already*. God has already put us in Christ. "But of him [God] are ye in Christ Jesus, who of God is made unto us wisdom, and righteousness, and sanctification, and redemption" (I Corinthians 1:30).

We are in Christ. There is nothing more we have to do to get there; nor do we have to worry about "falling out of Him." Any problems we may encounter with this arise because we do not clearly see and rely upon the fact that we *are* forever in Christ. We are tricked by the feeling that we must do something with, for, or of self. That feeling is a temptation of the flesh (James 1:14), just as Peter was tempted by the waves and faltered.

If the illusory self does not count for us, why mess with it any longer? Its best fruit is only wood, hay, and stubble, which will be consumed by fire in the day of the Lord (1 Corinthians 3:11-13). When we constantly analyze our "fruit," it is simply self worrying over self, which is always worried about its appearance. That leads to the Romans 7 syndrome. Then we feel forced to fix it up, rather than just leave it behind. "What will a man gain by winning the whole world, at the cost of his true self?" (Luke 9:25 NEB). However, a long time lack of the real fruit of the spirit is an infallible sign that we are identifying with the old "me" and its needs.

Sewing Our Leaves Together

There will be occasions, of course, when we are overtaken by sin and lend our body to it, especially in the beginning of our walk when the cross is not yet clear to us. Many times, before the cross becomes clear, in order to preserve our self-esteem we try to blame our failure on other things, other people, or even demons. It is very popular in some circles to blame the cause of our own sin on demons, or, as the popular phrase puts it, to say, "The devil made me do it."

If we think the old "me" is our identity we will desire to save our self. We will wish to preserve this self-image more than we want our true life and fellowship with God in liberty, and we will go the route of blaming externals for these sins. When God questioned Eve in the garden, her reply was, "The serpent beguiled me, and I did eat" (Genesis 3:I3).

It is true that the serpent deceived her, just as sin in the flesh will deceive us, but still she felt forced to hide herself. Had her answer truly satisfied her, she would not have still felt the need to hide. When we blame our sins on others, we too must hide: hide from ourselves and God, rather than face the facts and renew our conscious fellowship with Him. What we often label "demons" simply turns out to be the lusts spawned by of our own false self. "Temptation is the pull of man's own evil thoughts and wishes" (James 1:14 LB).

God's method is not just to remove the temptation so that we can have peace. His method is, instead, to remove *us* through the cross and to put Jesus (our true life) in place of the false identity "me." That does not remove the temptation, but it takes us out of the way and puts Jesus there in our stead. And Jesus cannot be moved.

When we do not understand the cross, we will bypass it to save self; we will try to remove the "demon," or the temptation, rather than take up the cross. But the only way for the soul truly to experience freedom from sin as God has intended is to see what God has provided through the cross of Christ for us, especially in times of our own failure.

"... if we walk in the light, as he is in the light, we have fellowship one with another, and the blood of Jesus Christ his Son cleanseth us from all sin" (1 John 1:7). Have you ever wondered what "walking in the light" means? This writer once had a lot of trouble with that, but found another very important verse which helped clarify it: "In Him was life; and the life was the light of men" (John 1:4).

The light which we are to walk in is Christ, who is *the light of awareness. Our pure awareness. But not what we are aware OF.* By living His life on earth He showed us what the true life was like so that we, through the cross, could always count on that life, rather than the old, imaginary self. He satisfies and illuminates us with Himself.

Walking in the light, then, is first seeing that Jesus is our light of awareness and relying on our oneness with Christ through the cross, because He, rather than self, is our true identity; and then also being honest about our own conduct in the body in comparison to our position in Christ. (Remember we are free from the law through the body of Christ.) Jesus continually cleanses us from all sin. Christ exchanges Himself for ourselves. "For he hath made him to be sin for us, who knew no sin; that we might be made the righteousness of God in him" (2 Corinthians 5:21). If we truly understand our freedom from the law through the body of Christ (Romans 7 Syndrome), it should be easy, then, to acknowledge and confess sins done in the body, for they are not imputed to us because of the death and Resurrection of Jesus Christ. We no longer have to protect the self-image but sins may still have consequences in the world.

It should be remembered here that God's desire is, above all, for us to know and participate in Him and live a joyfull, abundant life. He is not concerned with our earning His love, for what can a dead (in Christ) person earn, anyway? He already loves us, has chosen us, has bought our soul from hell at a great price, and now desires for us to be with Him experientially. There is no need for us to impress Him, as He loves us anyway. God's love does not depend on what we do or think. We have it simply because we are His.

Sin, using the law, will try to make us look at ourselves and try to fix it up. "For the law is the strength of sin." (1 Corinthians 15:56) As we have seen, God's way of dealing with this is not to fix up ourselves, but to remind us that He counts us dead and therefore beyond the law's requirements. Then He reminds us of our true life, the already perfect Jesus Christ. He died for us, and now lives for us. We died with Him, and now live in Him. When we rely upon that, we walk in the light.

But when we do not rely upon that, we walk in darkness. We are instead identifying with and relying upon the old, imaginary self and feel obliged to take care of it; we then think of Christ and ourselves as two separate lives, rather than one. The result is that "we lie, and do not the truth" (1 John 1:6).

If we want God's fellowship and reality more than the darkness and deceit of self, we turn from our own "righteousness" (that is, trying to justify and protect self), and turn to Him. "If we confess our sins, he is faithful and just to forgive us our sins, and to cleanse us from all unrighteousness. If we say that we have not sinned, we make him a liar, and his word is not in us" (1 John 1:9, 10).

When we are trying to cover up for self, we will try to say that we have not sinned, or will try to shift the blame elsewhere, or will try to rationalize our sin in such a manner as to prove that we had no choice. In trying to protect themselves, Adam blamed Eve, and she in turn blamed the serpent (Genesis 3:13).

We sin because we think that we have to. We do indeed have to if we are identifying with self, because then we feel the need to protect and satisfy it. But when we do so, we deny Christ's work on the cross and promptly "make him a liar, and his word is not in us" (1 John 1:10). Then we find that our total concern is on the false-identity, self. The result is that we walk in darkness and are enslaved by sin.

Our old nature will never lead us to find out its true character. It will only lead us in circles and darkness, because its real problem is that its very existence is based on imagination, illusion and lies. Self would never admit to that, for the truth is death to it. It will, instead, always find other reasons for why things are as they are.

Self's innate trickery is responsible for the fact that psychiatry and psychology have evolved into such complex mazes of knowledge. Those theories are like a house with many rooms tacked on here and there to take care of all the different situations. Psychiatrists and psychologists, while believing that they are gaining more knowledge, are only being led further and further into this maze, which is endless.

Their attempts to untangle the secrets of the old nature are like trying to find the end of a piece of string which is tangled into a huge ball, without knowing that the string is in fact a loop. There are no ends. We can trace things in our self forever, but we will only get more lost.

If we call these manifestations of the old self demons, we will then find an endless supply of them to cast out and an equally endless stream of more incredible explanations for why they keep coming back or why more are always showing up. Incalculable pain and confusion have been spread by such doctrines. Those who indulge in it are actually caught by the very one they feared most, Satan. But not by "demons;" only by Satan's lies which are successful in keeping them separated from the person of God, the cross of Christ, true deliverance, and the kingdom of God. Instead they are hopelessly bound up in their own self, their fights with Satan, their religious self-image, and all that goes with the old self. If one is still ignorant or doesn't believe in the full work of the cross, he will then be still participating in the old self and trying to clean out all the bad. And since it is of Satan, it truly is vulnerable to the powers of darkness, but we can't cast self out of self by self. There are demons, and they can be cast out, though such cases are not so numerous. But, then again, demons can only be involved with the old creation and the old false life and consequently only those who do not regard Christ as their life are vulnerable. "Did you not die with Christ and pass beyond reach of the elemental spirits of the world?" (Colossians 2:20 NEB). A Christian's answer to liberty is the cross of Christ. That is what the New Testament is all about.

When we understand and believe that Christ is our life, then we will find that our concern is on God and our experience is freedom. We will be walking in the light and in the kingdom of God.

When Adam and Eve's eyes were opened (Genesis 3:7), they turned their gaze inward and saw only emptiness. They knew that they were separated from their true identity in God, they were incomplete and exposed; then, because they identified with the body/mind as themselves, felt the need to sew leaves together to cover themselves. This is symbolic of other things as well. If we do not depend on our oneness with God in Christ, we, too, are incomplete, and feel the need to cover ourselves. Then the soul makes up its own covering "me," just as Adam and Eve made up their own flimsy covering of leaves. We feel that we need protection and covering just as Adam and Eve did in the Garden of Eden. However, oddly enough, even after Adam and Eve sewed together leaves (each leaf represents a facet of our self-image), they still had to go hide behind the bushes. So also when we identify with self, we feel the need to hide from the true God behind our spiritual images.

When we employ a spiritual image, we try to be "self-existent ones" (Exodus 33:19) or "as gods, knowing good and evil" (Genesis 3:5). We then project our own sin nature onto God, making Him to be as petty as we are, and we try to prove ourselves worthy of His love. We forget that "while we were yet sinners, Christ died for us" (Romans 5:8), and that "Herein is love, not that we loved God, but that he loved us" (1 John 4:10). We cannot stop His love for us, but we can refuse to accept it.

We forget that He sees all and knows our thoughts before we even think them. There is nothing we can hide from Him. When we desire Him and trust in His love and unchanging life, we can hold all things out before Him. God knew what Adam had done, but He still came to walk with him in the garden. We can stand in His light unashamed and unafraid because we are relying, not upon our righteousness or lack of it – we are counted as dead in Christ – we are depending on Christ's righteousness. This is symbolized when God Himself covered Adam and Eve with the skin of an animal (a slain lamb possibly?).

We are favored, not because we deserve it, but because we are in His Son, the favored one. We also are worthy, not because of our worth, but because we are in His Son, the worthy One. We are counted as one with Him, as the same as Him. We do not have to worry about our image before God, for the old self is counted dead and by His grace He has made us accepted *in* the Beloved (Ephesians 1:6). This is not so that we can be irreverent, but so that all barriers can be removed, and we can know Him from Himself.

Too often our notion of a Christian living a righteous life is one who is constantly preoccupied with avoiding sin. However, when we are concerned with not sinning, we have to watch ourselves all the time to make sure that we do not sin. We then have simply no time left to look at God. The law forces us to look at ourselves; but it is grace that enables us to look at God.

The Apostle Paul said that, "If we believe not, yet He abideth faithful: He cannot deny Himself (2 Timothy 2:13). He continues to be Himself, regardless of our actions in the body. He never leaves us or casts us out of Him, whether we are always consciously relying upon Him or not. He continues to be our true life, whether or not we are always acknowledging Him to be so.

As Christians we are always positionally in Christ, and cannot "fall out" of Him. God put us in Him when He was crucified (1 Corinthians 1:30); baptism acknowledges that fact. We are living positionally in Him, whether we are experiencing Him and walking in Him or not. Therefore, "If we live in the Spirit, let us also walk in the Spirit"(Galatians 5:25).

Many times when we regard the old self instead of Christ, we sometimes feel that He is gone or that we are not still in Him. But the fact that we have turned our gaze from the chair that we are sitting in does not mean that it is gone. If we turn our gaze to it and acknowledge it once again, we will see that it is still there.

When we regard the old self instead of Christ, we may not see Him or feel Him, but He certainly has not gone; nor have we. It does not mean that our life is not still in Him. We can at any time acknowledge that fact and continue resting in Him, for the false self is a *product* of the mind as imagination. At the fall it took on the role of "me." It just seems like it is you because the mind has that habitual belief. It must, therefore, be reconditioned or "transformed by the renewing of the mind." (Romans 12:12)

At night when we sleep we may dream that we are someone else, somewhere else. Possibly we dream we are in great peril. We may truly feel this and believe this in our dream but the *fact* is that we are still safe at home in bed and things haven't really changed one bit. When the day comes, we wake up and realize what has been truth all night. When we *know* that we are safe in our beds, we can truly rest there. Thus, a Christian may sometimes identify with the "dream person," the false self, which is always in great peril. We may truly feel self and believe it, but the marvelous *fact* is that the false imaginary self is not our real life, it is totally imaginary. We are still safe at home in heaven *in Christ,* and eternal things haven't really changed one bit. The day has come with the good news of Christ and we may now wake up and realize what has been truth all night. When we know that we are safe in Christ, we can truly rest there and participate in His life rather than the imaginary self life.

"And that, knowing the time, that now it is high time to awake out of sleep: for now is our salvation nearer than when we believed. The night is far spent, the day is at hand: let us therefore cast off the works of darkness, and let us put on the armor of light" (Romans 13:11, 12).

Many people go through much unnecessary misery because they miss that simple fact. For instance, instead of relying upon the fact that God has forgiven them, they insist upon wanting to feel forgiven. Actually they really want self to feel forgiven, but it can't, because it hasn't been. It is the *soul* that is cleansed by the blood of Christ from the contamination of the old dead self. It is an established fact that He took our sins and sin nature upon Himself two thousand years ago. Since He has already taken them, all we need do is simply acknowledge the sins we are aware of and gladly rely on that fact. What He has promised is always already a fact in the eternal now, whether yet revealed in time or not. We do not have to plead and bargain with Him or try to trick Him into forgiving us, because He has actually already done it. When we can acknowledge where we are and turn to Him, we can ask for and accept that forgiveness. Our feelings may fluctuate; indeed they undoubtedly will, but we can rely upon previously established facts which will never change. Our basis is not our own rationalizations, but the fact of Jesus and His sacrifice.

All of the previous things will lead us to discover a few more things: 1) When we rely on the facts rather than our feelings, all those previously desired feelings usually begin to follow along. 2) But even if they do not, the facts remain unshaken and, therefore, so can we. 3) To confess our sins and repent is to turn from regarding the false self, back into reality, because the fact that Christ is our life is reality.

His life is reality; His love is reality; His being is reality; His truth is reality; His way is reality. We rely not upon our work, but upon *His* work. When we rely upon His work, our work will line up. But if our faith is in our own work, we will never line up with Him. Rather than trying to get our lives to line up with His so that we can have fellowship with Him, we find that our life will spontaneously begin to line up with His *because* we have true fellowship with Him by faith in His work on the cross. The first way is bondage; the second is liberty.

The former way is law, which says, "Do, and you shall live;" the latter way is grace, which says, "Live, and because you live you shall spontaneously do." Law says "do," but grace says "done." We are counting, not upon what we do in order to deserve fellowship with God, but upon what has already been done for us to make possible that fellowship with Him and in Him.

He wants us first. If we are participating in Him, our lives in the body will reflect Him. It does not happen the other way around. We do not have to make up for what we have lost when we sin. We must only acknowledge and rely; there is nothing else necessary.

Christ is the truth, the fact. In Him there is no variableness or shadow of turning (James 1:17; Hebrews 13:8). Life eternal is not just for us to show off a superior life. Jesus said to the Father that, "This is life eternal, that they might know thee, the only true God, and Jesus Christ, whom thou hast sent." (John 17:3)

Temptation Can Be Used To Your Good

Temptation is to us just what the waves were to Peter. Our flesh will constantly give us different thoughts and feelings which shout that something there needs our attention. These are solicitations, enticements, or, if you will, advertisements to evil. But we can use them to walk upon to "go to Jesus" (Matthew 14:29) as Peter did.

Temptations need· not be desires for obvious sin, but for something which is just enough to put our attention on our imaginary self. Then our eyes are off Christ. That is all it takes. Then sin can do with us what it will. In James 1 we see that temptation is enticement of *our own lusts,* which are of the flesh.

We can now learn how temptation, instead of being miserable, can be a joy: Look at what these waves did for Peter. He used them to walk to Jesus! Does that sound impossible? It isn't. It is even scriptural. James said, "... count it all joy when ye fall into divers temptations" (James 1:2). A little later he said that we are blessed when we endure temptation, for we will receive a crown of life (James 1:12).

What does this mean? Does it mean gritting our teeth and holding on in willpower when we are tempted? So that when we die and go to heaven we will get a reward by and by? Is this how Peter walked on the water? *Not at all. Temptation can be used to lift us right to God,* right now, so that we can experience *His* very life and participate in Him. He is our reward. He is our treasure.

To see this we must first understand what it means to be *in Christ:* what it means to be dead in Christ as well as to be alive in Christ. If this is not clear to anyone, perhaps they can refer again to earlier chapters of this book before going on.

Sin uses the *familiarity* or conditioned reflexes of the old self to draw us into regarding it. If we do regard self, as it has been our custom for so long to do, sin can then use our bodies to express itself. That is temptation. The Holy Spirit will comfort and remind us that only what Christ is and does can count for what we are and do. As we abide in the truth, the truth will become more familiar than the lie (self) and each time we agree with the truth, sin has less power and less chance to express itself through us. "And be renewed in the spirit of your mind" (Ephesians 4:23).

The main job of temptation is to get us to turn from relying upon and resting in Christ and His finished work, and thus to *consider self.* This is the decisive factor. The Holy Spirit says, "You are in Christ. He is always your life." Temptation says, "You had better take care of this need that you (self) have." But if we know the truth we are free. If we know we are in Christ, we will rest in Him. We will know temptation's thoughts are irrelevant. The process is very much like ignoring irrelevant television commercials. It happens without trying when we know the truth.

We may have unchristian like thoughts, lusts, and desires; then other thoughts will rush in, condemning us for thinking the first thoughts (first lust, then the law to activate self). Our tendency is to believe that the first thoughts come from our flesh and the next from God, but that is untrue. They all come from the same place. And if we try to *do* anything other than rest in Christ, we sink as Peter did.

These desires and condemnations are of the familiar old self, and are designed to get us to respond to *it,* and leave the ground of liberty in Christ. Their purpose is to get us to act of our self and-for ourselves. God will give us wisdom in this, but only in accordance with our desire to *know* Him and abide in Christ. If our motive is just to appear sinless, we will only become confused and in further bondage. "A double minded man is unstable in all his ways" (James 1:8).

Here is the most wonderful part. When each temptation comes, it gives us the chance to regard consciously our position in Christ, to agree that *He* is our life. He is not tempted; if *self* is tempted, what has that to do with us? Christ-not self-is our life.

Self is weak and powerless, but Christ is not even moved. He is solid as a rock. He "was in all points tempted like as we are, yet without sin" (Hebrews 4:I5).

We need not drum up the willpower to try to keep self from succumbing to temptation. All we need do is recognize that self is outside and apart from us, and no longer one with us. We do not have to consider self's feelings and power, nor its bondage to the law. All we have to consider is Christ our life. His feelings and power are all that we really have or need. And remember, if and when you do sin, it has already been taken care of and is not counted as you or yours.

You Can Fly

In the next few paragraphs are some examples of how the familiarities of the old self tempt us into employing our members for sin. And how we, by the Holy Spirit, can use these occasions as an opportunity to know Christ and the power of His Resurrection. "I press on toward the goal to win the [supreme and heavenly] prize to which God in Christ Jesus is calling us upward" (Philippians 3:I4 AMPLIFIED).

It is always the old self with its petty vanity that gets offended and hurt. If the situation has not disturbed Jesus then it has not really disturbed us, for He is our *true* life. There is, therefore, no longer any place or reason for animosity.

The old self is always pursuing happiness, but never quite attains it. We will find that we *already* have the real happiness in Christ. The old self always chases the counterfeit and the fleeting, because it is counterfeit and fleeting. We know Christ is happy and content with the Father; then so are we in Him, not because things always go right for self, but because Jesus is the I AM. So we can give up participating in the old imaginary self's frantic chase for happiness and rest in Christ's happiness by faith.

Because we know the old self so well and have participated with it all our earthly lives, it feels familiar and comfortable. Many souls will not give up the old nature, even though it is a prison, because they fear that the loss of that identity means oblivion. Actually it is just the other way around. The old imaginary self has *already* been condemned to destruction at Christ's Crucifixion and, because it was imaginary, only Christ remains as our life. If we cling to the old self we pass up what is already ours (reality) in preference to a lie that we can never really have (Romans 1:2-25).

That is why some people even hate to leave behind an obviously foul self-because they feel that at least with it they are "somebody." Even if they are rotten, at least it is an identity and they think that their very rottenness proves them to be a man, etc. The Pharisees would not leave their old self because they had spent so much effort to get it "right," and were too involved with keeping it that way to really understand Jesus. But Jesus said, "Whoever cares for his own safety is lost; but if a man will let himself be lost for my sake, he will find his true self. What will a man gain by winning the whole world, at the cost of his true self? Or what can he give that will buy that self back?" (Matthew 16:25, 26 NEB).

The old self will always tell us that we are (it is) not fulfilled because we need more money, success, fame, power, recognition, consideration, sex, etc. That is because the old self will *always* blame externals rather than its own dreadful condition as the root of the problem. The imaginary self is always lacking substance and always will because it is built on imagination. Often our feelings will be coming from the familiar old self, tempting us to lend our faculties to it so sin can express itself through our faculties. However, since we are not bound to it anymore, its condition and needs are no longer of any concern to us. We know that our real identity in Christ is well and holy whether we feel it is or not. Our true self doesn't ceaselessly shift and change as does the old self. No longer do we have to go by changing, unpredictable, and often deceitful feelings to determine our real condition as we have been accustomed. Now we can go by the sure *knowledge* of Christ, the unchangeable One. He is our very sense of "I am," pure awareness.

The old self reacts out of conditioned habit for its own preservation. Our new life, Christ, spontaneously and without effort, follows the will of God out of love.

One of the most common tricks of the mind is a picture consisting of three separate entities labeled *Jesus, me,* and *self.* We will feel that once we get *me* disentangled from *self,* then *me* can be free to enjoy Jesus and a holy walk. We will feel that *Jesus* and *me* are the good guys, and *self* is the villain preying on innocent but weak *me.* But somehow we never seem to become completely free of self's attacks, no matter what spiritual techniques we use. This can go on indefinitely. We can be brought into deep despair unless we come to realize that *me* and *self* are not two, but one and the same. We may have guessed it. The mind has graciously presented us with "*me*" to identify with, instead of Christ, and blamed our problems on that boogieman *self.* Only the trouble is that "*me*" is still self in disguise, and is just as controlled by sin as ever. We will have to include "*me*" in with the old creation that was made null and void on the cross. We are left once again with just Jesus. Remember, it's not me, myself, or I plus Jesus, it's just *Jesus.* He is the one and only Life. We were created in Him and our real existence is in Him only. I am, but there is no "me."

Upon reading of how a true saint or spiritual person acts, we may be tempted to copy him. This is, in Jesus' words, "whitewashing the sepulcher." This is done from the motives created by the imaginary self, and is all backwards. We think that the outward appearance proves the inner reality, but remember the whitewashed sepulcher. This can cause us to try to skip the inner reality and bypass the cross for the sake of appearance. When we do this, we hope by outward appearance to change our inner life, or perhaps convince ourselves that we are not so bad after all. Possibly we are so aware of the hopelessness of our inner life that we ignore it altogether. Whatever the case, we are forgetting that our actions are the *result,* not the *cause,* of our personal relationship and oneness with God through Jesus Christ. Christ was not made one with God because He performed divine deeds; He performed divine deeds *because* He was one with God. If we would believe this and rely on it, we would be saved much frustration and condemnation. When God gave instructions for building the temple, He did not start from the outer fence and work inward. He started with the innermost part, the ark, and worked out from there. God always begins with Himself and with the interior. The outer then reflects the interior. "Taking up the cross," is not a burdensome, difficult thing. It is simply acknowledging that the old self is gone and our real life is Christ.

Are we thrown by the unexpected? Are we overcome by disappointments, changes in plans, sudden problems? Since self functions by previously learned habits of acting, it is thrown by the unexpected. It falls apart when things occur contrary to its anticipations. Self, like a petty god, wants to know what to expect, so that it will know how to handle the situation. Otherwise, it will be taken by surprise and exposed as inadequate. But Christ needs none of that. He is never surprised or damaged by unexpected events, whether or not they seem disastrous. And because He is our life, we are the same in Him through all occurrences, whether we are surprised or not. Christ is able to just let things happen if necessary. The Holy Spirit will guide us in this.

Many people think that if they can *feel* guilty enough for a sin, then they can pay for the sin or somehow stop themselves from sinning again. This is only a form of self-punishment, an attempt to do penance. And it participates with the old imaginary self. This kind of guilt is false. There can never be enough guilt to pay for even the smallest sin. Only Jesus could pay the price, and He has already done that with His blood. There is no sin we could in ourselves pay for, and there is no sin of ours that Jesus' blood has not already erased. He also has already borne our guilt. The only kind of guilt which will do us any good is a simple, honest acknowledgment that we have been participating with the old illusory self, instead of abiding in Christ where we really are. This is called conviction, and it comes to show us that we can turn away from self and rest in Jesus. Self-condemnation has no place in Christianity. "There is therefore, now no condemnation to them which are in Christ Jesus" (Romans 8:1). Guilt is the result of not believing in the efficacy of the blood of Jesus Christ. It is sin-controlled self's way of avoiding the cross, and keeping you prisoner by condemnation. Godly sorrow leads to repentance.

The Lord is our high tower. Even in the midst of confusion and hubbub we are separated from it all because we are in heavenly places in Christ, our life. We will be aware of self's confusion and problems, but we are not caught in them. We can depend on Christ, our true life, to do what is proper by the Holy Spirit. This is not egotistical aloofness, or a way of hiding our head in the sand, but is rather the only way to objectively face reality.

This is the only real way to be detached from strong negative emotions. Here again it is always the false self that has the fearful negative feelings. As we begin to understand the cross we will realize that there is no more need to fight against these negative emotions to try to make them stop bothering us. Fighting against them only seems to give them more power because we are then wrongly identifying those feelings as us and ours and consequently identifying with the false self they live in. This is actually part of the Romans 7 Syndrome. Christ, not our feelings, is our true life and we know that He is not threatened or fearful. He overcame death, sin, and Satan. He is the same yesterday, today, and forever. When we know this we can simply sit by in Him and observe those *emotions* and *thoughts* as they play upon the false self, while we, in Christ, are detached from them by the cross. The feelings still may be present in our body and the thoughts may still flit through our minds, but you are not your mind by virtue of Christ's work. Thoughts cannot actually touch or be a part of our true self, Christ. There is no need or way to join the old self in a fight against these feelings and thoughts because they have no real connection to us. Whatever difficulties the old false self has with those emotions and thoughts does not affect our true life, Christ, and therefore we are not involved in them. We can calmly watch them as we would watch a movie about some fictitious character, knowing that it is not real life. Only Christ is real life.

We cannot even use the exchanged life to make those negative feelings and thoughts stop. That is again only identifying with the false self that has caused the feelings. We are accustomed to thinking that when the feelings come we are in trouble and that when they leave it means that we are once again okay. But the mind is not our self, thinking. The cross is not meant to give the false self good feelings; it goes much deeper. It is meant to bring us to God and His real kingdom. The Bible says that negative feelings will be around till the end of the age, but that through Christ we can be detached or separated from them. He liberated us from the self that has those difficulties. “Peace is my parting gift to you, my own peace, such as the world cannot give. Set your troubled hearts at rest, and banish your fears” (John 14:27 NEB). “I have told you all this so that in me you may find peace: In the world you will have trouble. But courage! The victory is mine; I have conquered the world.” (John 16:33 NEB) Therefore it is no concern of ours whether these negatives are caused by the old, imaginary creature or not. They have no real power or effect on our real life. They are just part of the old creation which was made void in Christ.

The clearer the cross becomes, the further from us the false self and all its hang-ups seem to be. If we are unconsciously trying to use the cross to straighten out and gratify the false self, we will only run deeper into a maze of confusion and frustration. The cross is to sanctify or set us apart unto God from that old self, not to pacify it. The gospel is to tell us which of the two lives we can count as ours. This is to be known in experience as well, as it is a fact in eternity.

To sum it up: When negative thoughts and emotions pass through us we don't need to fight against them. Instead, we calmly rest in Christ and observe them as they play their games in the false self. And remember, they are not our thoughts and emotions. We are just spectators and free of the need to participate. "... the truth shall make you free." (John 8:32) "... but those who look to the Lord will win new strength, they will grow wings like eagles; they will run and not be weary, they will march on and never grow faint" (Isaiah 40:31 NEB). That's what we're created to do.

There was a young man in one of our study groups who was coming into an understanding of the exchanged life and was naturally quite excited about it. But then he began to run into the most awful defeat and confusion. One night he said to me half angrily, "Yes, I believe all that you're telling me and I know that it also says it in the Bible, but what's the *practical application* of it? It never works for me and now I feel even worse off than before." After talking with him a short time, I asked him if he might be seeing the exchanged life as something to be used for the advantage of the false self rather than the way for the mind to be able to leave that imaginary self, whatever its condition or emotional state, and spend its time with Christ in the kingdom. He got the strangest look on his face as he began to realize his mistake. I explained to him that the false self "knows" that the cross is death to it, so will instead try to twist it slightly and appropriate it for its own use. But the exchanged life can't really be used of the false self and only multiplies its frustration. This often brings us to write off the exchanged life as unworkable (as it is unworkable to the false self). In many lives sin often succeeds at this point in turning a soul back, and then it gives you more attractive, worldly religious principles that satisfy the false self, but only give the illusion of spiritual progress. Thus the kingdom is never seen.

Later the young man said, "Thanks for pointing that out. I see now that it is not a matter of me applying anything, it is just realizing what already *is* and seeing what is already done. It does not require anything else from me, and if I do find myself trying to use or appropriate anything, I know that it is only the old false self trying to appropriate things out of God for its own use. The cross is really the way for the soul to rest in God Himself and His eternal reality. Before it all seemed so complicated, but now I see that it is really very simple. It really is literally the truth itself that sets me free, instead of my own mental ability to keep the false self-pacified. From now on I know my Christian life will be much simpler, more joyous, more stable, and more honest. It is so much more than I'd even hoped for or thought possible. That's really the good news!"

Resting in Christ should happen spontaneously when we fully recognize what Jesus accomplished on the cross. We can find many more opportunities such as these to depend on our position in the risen Christ. We will find these opportunities in everyday situations and circumstances. Ordinarily many circumstances would be frustrating, but we can now see them as an adventure. God gives us the chance to rest in Him and discover more of Him and consequently our life in His kingdom.

The word *fruit* in "the fruit of the Spirit" (Galatians 5:22) is singular. This is because it is one life (Christ) that lives, not many separate virtues that are parceled out to us as separate fruits. If we are after separate virtues (or fruits), like patience, watch out! It's just the self image wanting to add virtues on in order to look good, rather than be left behind.

The result of resting in Christ is that we realize His person and the fruit of the Spirit appears in our actions. This should happen spontaneously. If we find that we are habitually continuing in sin, then we are not truly resting in Christ. This is always due to lack of a more complete illumination of Christ's finished work on the cross, not one's will power. The cross itself eliminates all goals other than God Himself. The cross itself, not our will, has the power to save us to the uttermost.

Let us always remember that we do not even have to get power out of Christ down to us. We are already in heaven with Him and in Him (Colossians 3:1-3). We and He are one; what is true of Him is now true of us. Thanks to Peter and his water-walking episode we also see now what James meant when he said, "Blessed is the man that endureth temptation: for when he is tried, he shall receive the crown of life (experiential knowledge of God), which the Lord hath promised to them that love him" (James 1:12). *That is liberty!*

7
Our Position is Meant to Be Depended On

"If we live in the Spirit, let us also walk in the Spirit."

Galatians 5:25

There is a story of a stout man arduously puffing his way up a long, steep hill. Presently an automobile approaches and stops next to him and the driver offers him a lift up the hill. He gladly accepts the ride, explaining how very weary he was, but then he does a very odd thing. Instead of sitting down in the automobile, he continues on in the same manner as before, walking up the hill. Only this time he is joyfully exclaiming how good it was to have been given the ride.

As ridiculous as this fellow may seem, he is no different than we often are. We gratefully accept our position in Christ, but often continue on in the same manner as before, without actually relying on what we have been given. Just as the stout fellow continued on foot when he needed to sit down in the car in order to experience the gift of a ride, so do we continue to live with the old imaginary self as our frame of reference instead of "sitting down" and resting in Christ. We need to actively count on our position of oneness in Christ before we can ever experience and participate in it. Let us not be content to substitute intellectual and theoretical interest in the position for the experiential knowledge, as the stout man did.

We can take this story even further and say that without the ride the stout man can never make it to the top of the hill. By taking the offer of a ride to be the end in itself, and continuing on foot (with his old self as frame of reference), he actually prevented himself from reaching his destination. We saw in the last chapter how Peter realized his position in Christ, then went on to experience and participate in it, also. We can see then how we can actually put a barrier between us and God by accepting the position in Christ as the end itself, without actually relying upon it (faith) to personally experience God in our hearts and lives.

The way we explore the kingdom might go something like this: God will often show us the next area of exploration by first giving us a hint that it might exist. Next He makes us curious about it. Third, He takes us to a mountain and shows this new land to us. Finally, He takes us down into it to explore it and participate in it

There are many who may approach the idea of our position in Christ; and the attitude is often, "That's great!" But then they just continue on living and thinking with the old dead self as the frame of reference. Theoretical knowledge of our position is not enough. The reason we are told of our true position in Christ is so that we can begin to reckon upon it, to think and live from that frame of reference. And the reason God wants us to reckon upon it is so that we can begin to know and participate in Him and His kingdom while still in the body!

The Shadow – Or The Reality?

This was the mistake many of the Jews made. They thought that sacrificing the animals properly and keeping the feasts were all that was necessary for their spiritual well-being. Jesus, the Life, the Word incarnate, tried to show them that the means were not the end, that all the ritual was only a shadow and form of the real thing: Himself and experiential union with Him. Likewise, Christian doctrine and liturgy is not the end in itself, but is merely a shadow of, and the means to, the real thing, which is God Himself.

Let's look at the Father and the world through Christ, instead of through self. The different frame of reference changes our attitude from dejection to joy. To have experienced knowledge of our oneness with God is the whole purpose of the Word and our subsequent Christian life. This is a genuine mystical experience. It is far beyond our "being a good witness," but something that is nevertheless intended for all Christians. All we have or need is Jesus Christ; by grace through faith in Him, we can experience God directly.

The fact that we believe certain things about God, and that we pray to Him, does not necessarily mean that we are participating in Him and experiencing Him directly. He has much more for us. These are only the means to an end. God Himself is that end. We can teach what He has done to bring us to Him, but we cannot teach Him; He can only be known by faith and in the Spirit. We can only participate in Him by actively counting on our position in Christ as those who are alive from the dead.

Indeed we cannot even reckon or count on our death and life in Christ until we have clearly comprehended the full work of the cross. It takes a Romans 7 experience to bring the full awareness of this to us.

Trying to reckon ourselves dead to sin and the law in Christ before we have received spiritual illumination of that fact (knowing: *see* Romans 6:6) will tie us in knots. We are in effect trying to make it real by believing instead of believing *because* it is real. Heaven is the real place; this world is just the shadow. We always get things switched around backwards. But this also comes as we (through a partial understanding of the cross and God's own drawing of our soul) *set our heart singly to know Him*. This desire is magnified and actualized as the full knowledge of Christ's work on the cross is known, and relied on. (Romans 6:6 and Philippians 3:10)

We cannot learn God. We can learn some things about Him, but knowing actual union with Him is different. We may expect certain fleshly feelings, thrills, and emotions, and we may get them. We might think it is God, but God has something for us far beyond that. Please, let's not get wound up in seeking *that* kind of experience. We are not· seeking experience itself, we are seeking *God Himself.* In fact, what we are talking about is not "religion," but a life altering recognition of what-we-are! This is beyond religion

In order to approach and be reconciled to God, we have to know and completely depend on what He has done. We cannot rule this out. God has gone to a great deal of trouble to make His finished work known to us. But when we get involved in it, we often forget the reason for it all, which is to experientially know God in liberty.

"That you may really come to know-practically, through experience for yourselves-the love of Christ, which far surpasses mere knowledge (without experience); that you may be filled (through all your being) unto all the fullness of God-[that is] may have the richest measure of the divine Presence, and become a body wholly filled and flooded with God Himself!"

Ephesians 3:19 AMPLIFIED

8

HOW DO I FIND GOD'S WILL FOR ME?

"A double minded man is unstable in all his ways."

James 1:8

Have we ever struggled with the problem of trying to determine God's will for ourselves, and found the answer to be unclear? We find ourselves going back and forth, considering this way and that; one scripture seems to agree with doing one thing, but another points to doing something entirely different.

We diligently seek a sign or some understanding concerning what we should do, but find none. Is God playing guessing games? Or, we wonder, has He perhaps already made His path very plain to see, and only our stupidity keeps us from finding it? Do we "step out in faith" and begin to carry out our decision, only to end up turning around and deciding that perhaps the other alternative was right after all?

This uncertainty seems to be common among many Christians. It would seem to come from a sincere desire to please God and do His will. Such a Christian wants so badly to do the things which would please God, and to refrain from those which would displease Him, that he becomes frozen, unable to move in any direction. He is so unsure of how to discern which ways are which, that he can accomplish nothing at all. Of course he finds this discouraging, and sometimes is plunged into despair all because he so anxiously desired to please God!

It seems very unfair that God would treat those children who truly wanted to please Him in this way. And surely He doesn't! Upon closer examination we find that such frantic indecision does not come from a great concern for God, but that just the opposite is true. In reality the concern is for our own flesh: whether it will be blessed, or will suffer. We seem to have the feeling that if we somehow second-guess God and go the right way, we will be blessed and escape God's displeasure and, more important, escape discomfort to the flesh (or damage to our "spiritual image").

This attitude just described, though seeming superficially to be conscientious and right, completely leaves out the fact of God's infinite love for us, the cross, and His undeserved favor to us through the Lord Jesus Christ. We are forgetting that God's deepest and main desire is that we should experience union with Him and know Him in liberty. All things in our life are ordered for *that one purpose.*

We don't need to always pray to God to make everything go right (we often do and it often doesn't), that is living by blessing and calamity. Jesus didn't spend long hours in prayer with the Father just to make sure everything would go well at the miracle session the next day. He didn't pray so that he wouldn't look silly because nothing worked. He didn't go to the Father to stay in His good graces in order to be a favored son. Just the opposite. He prayed a lot simply because He knew He was so beloved of the Father. He knew He *was* one in the Father-not in order to be and stay in the Father. Jesus didn't pray to get. He prayed because He knew He already had. He couldn't be kept away from the Father; they talked things over-Father-Son, not because He was "religious" or needed guidance and power (He was the Life, the Truth, the Way). All the Father had was already His; He loved the Father because He *knew* the Father and knew the Father loved Him. Our situation is no different than Jesus. Because of Christ's work on the cross there is no more us and Jesus, but just Jesus-we are in Him-no more two but one. We, in Christ, have that same relationship with the Father. If we only knew.

In constantly worrying over whether or not we are choosing "what God wants for us" and consequently the path of blessing, we show self's distrust of God's motives, and the belief that He is less than truly loving. This is the way self understands God. Under the guise of trying to please God, we are actually trying to please our flesh and use God to do it by choosing the least painful or "most spiritual" way. Thus, if we begin in one direction and don't immediately succeed, and run into difficulties, confusion, hardness on the flesh, we conclude that this in fact was not God's will for us after all; supposedly He is trying to stop us by making things difficult. So we abandon that path, thinking that God's hand is definitely not on us there and He wants us to turn back. Then we fear that surely we have lost ground with Him, because we have made the wrong choice.

The whole situation becomes much simpler when we know that God's *one* purpose for *every* situation in our life is *only* that we might know Him and life in Him. It is futile to read any other reason into any situation.

All this talk about God teaching us guidance, patience, and humility, etc. through our trials in seeking His will is the leaven of the Pharisees. It is more like divination than discernment. Notice that this kind of self-seeking Christianity only makes us more self-centered, only makes us better phonies, and hardens our hearts with false humility and will-worship. If we ever again wonder what God is trying to teach us in the middle of a dilemma we can be sure that it is not how to use our wits to handle it better next time, nor to fervently pray for guidance in order to avoid a feared calamity. He only wants us to see and depend on His person and work on the cross. Then situations won't matter because we will discover our true life in heaven. We will stop praying for deliverance when we see that by the cross we have already been delivered right out of everything into the kingdom of heaven. We must be reminded that the old self hasn't been delivered (only unto death). We are free from circumstances only in Christ. We will then find it possible to disregard the whining ambivalence of the flesh and the frantic search for "God's will" ceases.

"All I care for is to know Christ."

Philippians 3:10 NEB

Instead, we are able to enter into real communion with Him. Our thoughts and actions are directed not by the knowledge of good and evil (or the knowledge of blessing and calamity) (*see* Genesis 3:5), but by the spirit of life in Christ Jesus. There is no need for us to label things that happen to us or people, places, and events as fearful, terrible, or tragic. Since we are in Christ, these things cannot really be anything like that anymore. They can only work to our good now, as they give us the opportunity to actively count Christ as our life and to participate in Him.

It was, after all, a desire to "rush God" and "get the best blessing" that led Adam and Eve into separation from God and expulsion from the Garden of Eden (*see* Genesis 3). Our old nature seeks the knowledge of good and evil in precisely the same manner; its excuse may have changed to a "sincere desire for the Lord's will," but its real motives are the same.

But in communion with Christ, we find that, regardless of our decisions, whether extremely wise or foolish, "all things work together for good to them that love God, to them who are the called according to his purpose" (Romans 8:28). That does not say that all things *might* work to good if we figure them out, but that all things *do* work together for good. We can count on this (if the good we are after is Himself).

If, to us, *good* means the gratification (or improvement) of the old self, then all things work together for our destruction. But if, to us, *good* means an opportunity to realize in experience our oneness with God, the question of whether circumstances will be good to, or hard on, the flesh, becomes of no concern to us. If we see that God desires for us only to discover what we already have, union with Him in liberty, then we can thank Him truly for all things. All things become blessings whether they appear to self to be blessings or calamities.

Suffering is not to grind us down and make us give up our pride and selfishness, etc., or to improve and educate us so that we will display Christian virtues. Suffering is not to teach us Christian living. We are *dead!* We are, instead, given the living Christian, Christ. Suffering can only be used as an opportunity to discover and rest in *His* person and work. Anything else is vanity and insanity.

"The picture of the fruit you have *not* found is still for a moment before you. And if you wished – if it were possible to wish – you could keep it there. You could send your soul after the good you had *expected,* instead of turning it to the good you had got. You could refuse the real good, you could make the real fruit taste insipid by thinking of the other," said the Green Lady in *Perelandra* by C. S. Lewis. God is a calamity to the false self, but a blessing to the soul.

Note that one of Eve's major mistakes, before partaking of the fruit of the tree of the knowledge of good and evil, was doubting the loving kindness of God for her; she doubted that He was giving her His best, that she had the true good. She sought a different good. Her soul took it upon itself to leave the real good for a "good" she had in her own mind. We know the disastrous results.

Since Adam and Eve fell, man's desire has been to be "like unto the Most High God" (Lucifer-see Isaiah 14:14). But God's desire is to give us all of Himself if we but give up having to be *like* Him, which is really our imagination of Him.

At every moment, in every situation, no matter how it may appear, God is always giving us His best. When we discover that this is so, we will cease trying to determine

God's will for us through looking at blessing and calamity. Then amazing things begin to happen.

In believing that God's main desire is for us to know oneness with Him in Christ and His divine character, we can turn from our shifting old nature's reason, and by faith accept the sound fact of God's omnipotent power over circumstances, and His infinite love for us. We then find ourselves being led by the reason of the Holy Spirit without effort, without difficulty, whether we are a great theologian or not. The *only* real power for life unto God is not our own wits, but simple, childlike dependence on *God's* keeping power through Jesus Christ. This is walking in the Spirit.

God is much more interested in our *heart* than in our accomplishments. This is not fatalism or an excuse for passivity and carnality, nor does it condone license; indeed, just the opposite is true. If it is received in a heart that truly desires to know oneness with the person God in liberty, it will lead to the most active seizing of every opportunity to know the reality and nearness of God and glorify Him. We can count on the fact that His greatest desire is for us; if our desire is also truly for Him, then we can surely meet all situations in our life as being from God's hand. “If God be for us, who can be against us?” (Romans 8:31).

Many times we run into situations that are difficult and trying, and we trace their sources to unfortunate accidents, or to man's sin, or the devil's wiles. We then blame these freak things on chance, or men, or Satan, and find ourselves becoming bitter: angry at our brothers, angry at non-Christians, angry at change, angry at devils, and many times even angry at God. Christ, the true self, does not *have* to do anything that circumstances and other people do not permit. Christ is already content: without always *having* to do and to have. He is the I AM. Only the old nature becomes frustrated and cheated of gratification. We must not mistake a need to dominate others or to indulge in self as "accomplishing 'God's will." What God wills, He makes a way for. People cannot stop His will. We must not blame other people or circumstances for frustrating our plans to "do God's work." This leads only to self-pity, self-righteousness, and bitterness. And there is no profit there. Our actions would indicate that we think things sometimes get out of God's control and harm us before He has a chance to take care of them. Or that we feel unless we are continually treading on the right path, then some terrible misfortune will be allowed to overtake us. That is self's understanding of God-which incidentally is true from self's point of view-for self is God's enemy and therefore instinctively knows God is "out to get it." It can't trust Him.

Such fears reveal that, once again, we fail to realize that Christ is the life. We have forgotten God's omnipotence and the reach of His grace and loving kindness toward us, His children, whom He has placed in heavenly places in Christ Jesus. But God hasn't forgotten it. Nothing can ever, ever be allowed to happen to our bodies on the earth that God has not already known and permitted. However, it doesn’t mean we are to be a doormat for everyone to walk on. We will now spontaneously meet every circumstance with wisdom and joy, trusting that God will guide us.

We can say that everything that comes to us is predestinated from God. He is not making things up as He goes along. God is sovereign. *He is* the beginning and the end. He knows all things, and holds all together by the word of His power. And He is our true life. Incredible!

Therefore, even though a misfortune we encounter may originate in man's sin, it could never have touched us without God's express approval. By believing in God's omnipotence and desire for us to know and experience our true oneness with Him in Christ, we can see that all circumstances are designed for this main purpose. The Crucifixion of Christ is the best example of this.

If we want *Him,* then we can have the unlimited joy that comes from knowing our desire is also His desire, and all things are to lead us to apprehend and participate in this union. We can trust God in all things, and rejoice in all things. We can truly say, “Surely goodness and mercy shall follow me all the days of my life: and I will dwell in the house of the Lord forever" (Psalms 23:6).

When we see that God and our true life are one and the same, we are free from having to worry about how things will work out for "me" which is separate from God and other than the true self. We see that we have been worrying 'about the wrong person ("me"), who doesn't count for us, and have forgotten that Christ is our true life and Christ is in God. Every situation, then, that is labeled disastrous, disagreeable, or opposed to our old nature, will now be used by God to remind us that we are crucified unto the world and the world is crucified unto us through Jesus Christ. Thus in Christ there is no "blessing and calamity." We can count on the fact that Christ is our life. We can rest in Him: in who He is and what He is. So we may experience God, the power of God in our lives, and God's own rest and peace in our hearts. That is resurrection life! That is the kingdom of God!

When we see all things as coming from the hand of God, we see them differently than we do when we look at them (from the imaginary self) simply as man's mistakes. If we do not consider God's hand in our situations we find ourselves constantly trying to change man and circumstance, rather than picking up our cross, denying self, and experiencing God.

Where does all this leave us when it comes to daily living? Shall we try to use others and gratify ourselves, or shall we know God as our purpose and Christ as our life? Isn't the latter a lot simpler than trying to continually manage our old nature, manipulate other people's lives, and worry over circumstances around us?

We will find that the greatest control is in needing no control. That is liberty. In it we glorify God by trusting in Him. A strange and wonderful thing happens then: While abiding in Christ, we find that He also abides in us, and He handles the situations. By His own instinct and power in us, He manages not only us, but those things around us, according to the divine will of the Father. And, we might add, He takes care of them infinitely better than we did by taking thought or worrying over them.

9

Do We Want Knowledge or The Knowledge of the Truth?

"Pilate saith ... What is truth?"

John 18:38

In our own Christian walk, do some of us ever find that we keep learning new, interesting spiritual things that promise to be the answers to our problems, but they never-quite measure up to our needs? If so, we find ourselves periodically running from one teaching to the next, knowing that the new one will finally be the promised "answer." But suddenly our life is an accumulation of many complicated "spiritual truths" and little else.

When this happens, we tell ourselves that we are growing and maturing as Christians, but, deep down inside, something longs for that joy we had when we were first saved. We were sure then that we had the answer and needed nothing more. Have we heaped knowledge upon knowledge and yet found that all of it has not brought us to that rest for which our soul hungers and thirsts?

Paul told Timothy that in the last days men would be "Ever learning, and never able to come to the knowledge of the truth" (2 Timothy 3:7). Paul spoke of *the* knowledge of *the* truth, not a lot of knowledge of a lot of truths.

Many times we think that the answer is in knowledge itself. The world thinks that education is the cure-all for society, but things only become worse rather than better. A good education and sound knowledge of the Bible are certainly desirable, but the accumulation of knowledge for its own sake is futile.

Chasing after knowledge which will change our lives is often like chasing the end of the rainbow: always we find ourselves almost there, but we cannot quite close that last small gap. It seems to remain the same distance away no matter where we move; it is not quite within reach, but is close enough to lure us on.

Later in the same letter to Timothy, Paul foresaw that "...the time will come when they will not endure sound doctrine; but after their own lusts shall they heap to themselves teachers, having itching ears" (2 Timothy 4:3). This lust was the lust for knowledge, that final kernel of truth which would be "the answer."

The lust for knowledge lures us astray like bits of corn lead a wild fowl along the path to a trap. First the fowl spots one bit of corn a little way from the rest of the group; then it spots another, and another, and soon the bird is caught. Paul admonished the Ephesians not to walk "...as [the] Gentiles walk, in the vanity of their mind, Having the understanding darkened, being alienated from the life of God through the ignorance that is in them." (Ephesians 4:17, 18). To the Corinthians he said, "... the world by wisdom knew not God ..." (I Corinthians 1:21).

The tree of the knowledge of good and evil was "... a tree to be desired to make one wise ..." (Genesis 3:6). This desire for the knowledge of good and evil, or the knowledge of blessing and calamity, is part of our inheritance from Adam. Adam and Eve were hungry for it, and greedily ate. But they only became more hungry, and found themselves less full. Have we ever been jealous of someone who seems to have more "spiritual knowledge" than we? Are we ever eating, but unable to be full? That kind of hunger is of the old creature. It is a symptom of the need of our soul for a real life.

The old nature, being only an empty concept, is constantly hungry for something new, new things, new experiences, and new demands. However, when we get them, we may be happy for a while but the mind soon comes up with yet something else we need to be happy. And on and on it goes our whole life unless we discover this ruse.

"Ho, everyone that thirsteth, come ye to the waters, and he that hath no money; come ye, buy, and eat: yea, come, buy wine and milk without money and without price. Wherefore do ye spend money for that which is not bread? and your labor for that which satisfieth not? hearken diligently unto me, and eat ye that which is good, and let your soul delight itself in fatness. Incline your ear, and come unto me; hear, and your soul shall live; and I will make an everlasting covenant with you, even the sure mercies of David ... Seek ye the Lord while he may be found, call ye upon him while he is near" (Isaiah 55:1-3, 6).

Jesus is the fulfillment of the abundant promises given to the prophet Isaiah~ "... whosoever drinketh of the water that I shall give him shall never thirst; but the water that I shall give him shall be in him a well of water springing up into everlasting life" (John 4:14). "And Jesus said unto them, I am the bread of life: he that cometh to me shall never hunger: and he that believeth on me shall never thirst" (John 6:35).

Too often we confuse knowledge with the truth. Jesus said, "I am ... the truth" (John 14:6). The truth is a person. We are not saved by what we know, not even what we know about Him. We are saved by Him. We must know Him personally, and rely on His love, His life, who He is, not on what we are or what we know.

We count on the person God, not just some knowledge of what is right and what is wrong. If knowledge of doctrine could save us, then Satan himself would be saved, for he no doubt has a knowledge of Scripture and doctrine far superior to ours.

But Satan is turned away from the person of God. He is separated from the life and reality of God, and he wants to keep us that way also. Having all the knowledge in the world is no replacement for having a living, personal union with God, through Jesus Christ.

Many people, upon receiving the facts in this book, will try to live by principles and concepts. Please do not make this mistake. We live by a Person, Jesus. The difference is the difference between rest and frustration, between true walking in the Spirit and frantically trying to hold concepts in your head. Each contradiction and confusion of the world will try to make us scramble for the right principle to apply, but we do not apply principles. We are depending on a person who is our life. *He* is omnipotent, and He loves us. Even if we are confused and temporarily at a loss, He is not. We are in Him. He keeps us; we do not keep ourselves through mental gymnastics. In the world we needed our quick wit to protect self. We need not protect it anymore, if He is our life and new nature.

In an earlier chapter we touched on the verse where Jesus said, "Ye search the scriptures; for in *them* ye think ye have eternal life: and they are they which testify of me. And ye will not come to me, that ye might have life" (John 5:39, 40). Through an abundant accumulation of knowledge of what we today might call "Bible principles," the Pharisees were seeking to change or reprogram the old nature "me" to conform to a spiritual image. Christ's plea was to leave "me" altogether, not just its manifestations; as He, not a changed or more intelligent "me," was the food for a starving soul that can only find substance in the Person of God. When we first were saved, we probably did this. We came to a person.

We relied only upon who He is, and what He accomplished for us. That is why we had joy! That is why we had life! That is why we were filled! Paul gave very simple but good advice to the Colossians when he said, "As ye therefore received Christ Jesus the Lord, so walk ye in him" (Colossians 2:6).

True Christian growth is simply an increasing discovery that there is no one left who must "grow." The old imaginary self is dead and counted out while Christ the Life is already perfect. We participate in His perfection in knowing Him by faith. Then we notice the true fruit of the Spirit, but that is only the manifestation of what already is.

In praying to His Father, Jesus said, "And this is life eternal, that they might know [that is, perceive, recognize, become personally acquainted with] thee the only true God, and Jesus Christ, whom thou hast sent" (John 17:3). Life eternal is not a doctrine, but a union in love.

When we have doctrine apart from a love relationship with God, we (if the doctrine is true) perhaps have the means, but not the end itself. A. W. Tozer explained, "Christian truth is designed to lead us *to* God, not to serve as a substitute for God." God saved us simply for Himself, by Himself, to Himself, by recreating us in Himself through Jesus.

He saved us because He wanted our good, not because He wanted us to do things, or because he wanted to take things from us. He does not want just to use us, but simply to love us and do us good. When we begin to be curious about what *kind* of love God must have for us, something stirs within us.

When that curiosity grows into a single great desire to discover His person, we then finally, through the cross and blood of Jesus, enter in to experience the unique person God and His love. God promised that "... he is a rewarder of them that diligently seek him" (Hebrews 11:6). And what can that reward be but Himself: knowing Him. if we are looking for something, the greatest reward we could receive would be simply to find that for which we were looking. We will come to realize that what we are looking for is what is looking!

We may think that we have a personal relationship with Him because we have learned about Him and pray to Him. However, all His effort has been to open the way for us to *experience* Him directly by faith.

But so much of our time is often wasted on trying to assure ourselves and others of our spirituality and deep knowledge of God. We feel that He will favor us because of our *knowledge* rather than because of Christ. Even then we desire His favor, not for His friendship, but only for what we think we can get out of Him for self. Because we do not believe that God already favors us in Christ, and because we fear to appear as though God was not favoring us, we often try to protect self by building a spiritual image. We reel off glib doctrinal answers, but inside we are empty. Every wind of doctrine tosses us to and fro. All this lust for knowledge in itself is the thinking of the false self, "me," and not the thinking of our true self Christ. We need not identify with it. Even these thoughts, as well as self, are made void through Christ's death. They never were you or yours.

If we are eating of the tree of the know ledge of good and evil, it will never truly satisfy. It is illusion and illusion is not real and solid and filling. Eventually the soul must seek God for Himself.

Here's a hint to those who seek deeper understanding. Only when Adam and Eve became identified with their bodies as themselves could the knowledge of good and evil have any meaning for them.

Hidden Knowledge – Or God Himself!

In relation to the subject of knowledge, we often have a grave mistrust of God. Many times we think that He has hidden things from us, but the truth of the matter is that it is we who are blind. God did not hide His spiritual truth in the Bible for the clever to dig out through scholarly searching.

The problem is that we have been blinded through our own deceitfulness and impure motives. We project, although perhaps unknowingly, our own nature onto God. Since our fallen nature behaves in this manner, we feel that God must, also. And so we suspect that the Bible also is written in clever deceitfulness and through impure motives like our own.

Since Adam, religious man's desire is to be *like* Jesus or God ("I will be like the Most High") – (Satan, Isaiah 14:14). But God's desire is not to make our old selves *like* Him, but to *give us Himself, instead of* our old selves.

The person who is "seeking God" while still identifying with the self will know only self's Promethean concept of God, which again is accurate from self's point of view-just as a lie would like to have the same appearance as the truth, but in substance is its opposite. A lie must always be in jealous fear of the truth. Thus, the ambivalent, double-mindedness of a mind in bondage to its own invented self.

A soul bound to the lie of self seeks to appear as truth, a real person, by feeding on the knowledge of right and wrong, good and bad, etc., though all it will ever be is a real *lie.* The lie knows that the real Truth, the person God, will put it out; so it meticulously avoids the true person of God while seeking to know about Him in order to copy and use Him to its own ends. That is often the reason that we feel that God is most elusive when we think we are trying the hardest to find Him. We will be hampered in knowing God in direct proportion to its identification with self, as it cannot really know *Him* from self's point of view, neither will God show Himself. This is where the all too familiar word *repentance* comes in. It is not identifying with self, not giving up things, not trying to reform; it is a turning "upstream" or prior to, thoughts and concepts, to recognize the true person of God. In the former it has no lasting help from God, but in the latter we have all the love and power and mercy of the Godhead to assist us in our true response to our Father's love. Then you can say I am, but there is no "me."

God freely gives out of love. He is guileless. He is innocent. He is not the kind to hide things and make us do tricks to get them out of Him. When we make Him out to be devious like ourselves, we are seeking the wrong things from the wrong person. A spiritual knowledge and life-style come as a *result* of a personal relationship with God through the cross, not as a prerequisite to it. The first instance is grace; the second is law.

Liberty and grace say, "You have Me and My love and therefore you will be able to do this:" law and bondage say, "Do this and you will have Me and My love. "This attitude of "If you will get your spiritual knowledge and living style straight, then you can be friends with God," is one of the single most common errors in the church today. An astounding number of churches, books, etc., today teach this kind of "Christianity" though.

This religion is in essence a kind of forgiveness of sins for the old self (instead of death in Christ) combined with various methods of self-improvement and moral conduct based on, *scriptural principles, commands, and threats.* After reading the previous chapters of this book we should recognize this immediately as a method wherein the forgiveness of sins is taken by the self-centered mind to be a salvation *for* the old self. Thus we are still left in the weakness and bondage of self (the Romans 7 Syndrome) to attempt to forge a new, improved self-image through willpower, assisted by various so-called deeper principles of God and Bible commands coupled with admonishments and threats of calamity, either inferred or implicit.

It is deeply grieving that this kind of thing is passed off and accepted as orthodox Christianity today, because it is basically identical to the religion of the Pharisees of Christ's time.

We have, in this kind of religion, made forgiveness through the blood of Jesus into a kind of license for self and labeled it "grace," while continuing to identify with the self (because we think the old self has been "saved"). This is putting new wine into old wine skins and the new patch on the old garment that Christ spoke of in Matthew 9:16, 17. This leads to the necessity of balancing self on the other side with law or legalism to keep self from getting too far out of line with this "grace." Notice also that we are still preoccupied ultimately with ourselves. Even though God is appealed to and praised, it is all with an eye to how it will affect ourselves.

Next we see our present-day denominations arguing with each other over which commandments we can forget because of "grace" (license), and which we must keep in order to preserve a moral but edacious life-style. That is the cause behind all the splits, schisms, hatreds, and prideful sects in so-called Christianity today. We have the "Fightin' Fundies" on one end, the "Children of the Universe" on the other, with the majority in the middle trying to live a "balanced" Christian life by will power in the same old bondage in which they were born. All are still tightly in the grip of the law of sin and death, unable to overcome their own nature by their own nature.

But above all this running to and fro from law to license and trying to balance them somewhere in the middle, God has another law that will overcome the law of sin and death that grips our soul in darkness. It is called "the law of the Spirit of the life in Christ Jesus" (Romans 8:2) and comes into operation immediately when a weary soul turns from self to truly rest in Christ. To those still unknowingly abiding in the old creature who have twisted the words of Paul to have a lesser meaning, this will all sound like just so much more license, repression, and willpower. "... if our gospel be hid, it is hid to them that are lost: In whom the god of this world hath blinded the minds of them which believe not, lest the light of the glorious gospel of Christ, who is the image of God, should shine unto them" (2 Corinthians 4:3, 4). But those souls who have seen that self is not just the bad impulses, but what they thought was their very identity, are also the souls who see that the cross has already dealt with that false identity, the law that pertained to it, and all its images so that God can give them back real life; hidden to the world and self in God Himself.

Do we know now what Jesus meant when He said "Beware of the leaven of the Pharisees?" And do we now know why He kept saying it? Phariseeism is worrying about and trying to fix up or make holy the very person whom Christ has made void on the cross – "me." Grace is counting on a new life created and *hidden* with Christ in God. A new self created in righteousness and true holiness which is *other* than the one we know as us. The false self can counterfeit every genuine virtue. It fabricates a mirror image of the real thing. The counterfeit virtue is an act, a covering put on by self, a whiting of the sepulcher. The genuine virtue is simply what Christ is. When we participate in our imaginary self, the old nature, we can only live an imaginary life. Self consists only of counterfeit attitudes and false viewpoints. To really live we need a real life, which is Christ.

Too often we are taught to think of God as jealously guarding the best knowledge and provisions for Himself and for special obtainers. We then think that His blessings have to be coaxed and tricked out of Him by our fulfilling particular requirements, ostensibly because we need to prove to God that we are faithful and mature enough to handle all this secret knowledge and power.

We might as well be trick animals, who must go through amusing gyrations that we do not particularly enjoy before we may have a piece of sugar. We are told that, by doing these strange gymnastics, we will "grow and mature."

Perhaps this image of God the circus trainer seems true if we, while participating with the old self, are after just the blessing (the spiritual image, the knowledge of spiritual secrets, or the material provisions) rather than singly after God the person. When we are after the sugar for the old self, we end up chasing the end of the rainbow which leads to nowhere.

Thus we will go through a spiritual maze and try to perform all the right things to satisfy God of our faith and maturity. We may get our reward, but we will nevertheless end up worse than before and probably frustrated at God. “And he gave them their request; but sent leanness into their soul” (Psalms 106:15).

A classic example of this “Do first, and then you will receive” attitude comes around collection-plate time. We are told that if we give a little to God, He will give a lot back to us. However, it is up to us to start the ball rolling by giving to Him (meaning that particular church or preacher), so that God will know that we have “faith.” As if God didn’t already know our heart.

Another example is the teaching that before God can bless us with provisions, He must give us problems to nurture and test our maturity. These teachings are going on in many churches, but they are really no different from the old practice of selling indulgences or even the greedy get-rich-quick schemes promoted by unscrupulous businessmen. Such plans are designed to appeal to our own lusts, and so they do. If we are after the “provisions” we are bound to have problems. God Himself can be our only goal and Jesus Himself is the only way.

What do we want: a spiritual image for the old self, money and blessings; or to know the person God? If we want God, we do not buy Him off or purchase favors by putting money in the collection plate. If we want God, we do not suffer through problems in order to prepare us or prove our spirituality and get a provision. These attitudes are exactly backwards from God's intention for us; they are counterfeit.

God's promises are not at all dependent on our actions in this manner. What He promises is *already a fact* in the kingdom, whether manifestly revealed or not. He has *already* given Himself to us: If we want Him, we have Him.

We do not give in order to have; we give because we *already* have. He has already poured out His *all* for us on the cross. What more can there be than Almighty God Himself! We begin to enter into His love simply by believing that it *is*. We keep wanting Him to *run* our life, but He must *be* our life (new self). We keep wanting Him to give *provisions* to ourselves when He has *provided Himself* to be our true self.

Doesn't "Do the right thing for God, and you will get those provisions you want" sound very much like law? And doesn't it sound like instructions for a servant for hire? It is indeed. It is part of the old creation, and is the worst kind of bondage. It is just plain Phariseeism.

There is not even anyone to appropriate anything as our true life (Christ) is not apart from God, and *appropriate* connotes getting something out of something. When we want to appropriate something from God, we are identifying with self again and are living for an illusory self apart from God and wanting to give it God's attributes. Instead, let's live from our true life, Christ, who is *hidden* in God, and indeed is identifying with and included in *all* that God is.

The excuse, "God wants to give to us, but He cannot until we are mature enough to handle His gifts of riches, knowledge, and power" may sound a little better, but isn't it the same thing: law and bondage? That sort of thing only appeals to pride. Didn't Paul reveal the fallacy of it when He said that God "... hath [past tense] made us meet to be partakers of the inheritance of the saints in light... and hath [past tense] translated us into the kingdom of his dear Son" (Colossians 1:12, 13).

We can then ask once again, "Just what is our inheritance?" Remember, if we try to begin sorting out what God owes us and what we owe God, we are in danger of going again into bondage over wondering what we do to get ours. We are again ignoring the cross of Christ in recognizing two separate lives. We are counting the old creature as still being our life. However, because of Christ we and He are not two, but one.

He is the One who arranged for our inheritance; He is the One who is presently giving it to us. He did not intend for us to have to use His own Scripture to pry provisions out of Him, or away from the devil.

Not many earthly fathers would behave in this manner with their sons. Why, then, do we think that God would do so? Sometimes we slander God in this fashion because we (identified with self) are not so much interested in Him as in what He has that we can use.

Often we do not think of Him in such an unpleasant way because we hate God so much as because we have never really considered His person. The possibility that He just might be totally different from the way we have always "known Him" in self has never occurred to us.

The most wonderful discovery we can make is that He really is worth knowing *just for Himself.* Nothing apart from Him has any value at all, either to Him or to us. He does not give us gifts as enticements to be His friend. *He* is the gift.

He has been giving Himself to us for a long time. We are not able to see what He has been giving only because our values are different from His and our minds have for so long been in bondage to self. What, then, is our inheritance, but *He Himself!* What, then, belongs to Him, but *we ourselves?* He belongs to us *now;* we belong to Him *now.*

When the meaning and reality of this penetrate our heart, the result is devastating. We love Him, because He first loved us. We give ourselves to God in love, because He has first given Himself to us in love.

The other way around is backwards. We cannot through our deeds or efforts please God, because of the weakness of our old nature. It is inherently self-centered. God has a better plan for us. He sent His own Son in the likeness of human flesh, except that He was without sin, and He gave Himself for us, that sin's power over us might be destroyed (Romans 8:3).

Hannah Whitall Smith, in her book *The Christian's Secret of a Happy Life,* gives us an excellent picture of the difference between the two kinds of experience the Christian can have. She says that it is a fact beyond question that there are two kinds of Christian experience, one of which is an experience of bondage, and the other an experience of liberty.

In the first case the soul is controlled by a stern sense of duty, and obeys the law of God, either from fear of punishment or from expectation of wages. In the other case the controlling power is an inward life principle that works out, *by the force of its own motions or instincts,* the will of the Divine Life-Giver, without fear of punishment or hope of reward. In the first the Christian is a servant, and works for hire; in the second he is a son, and works for love.

We will experience bondage in one degree or another until God brings us to the place where He Himself, rather than what He can give us, is our sole love and interest. As Saint John of the Cross said, "For if you desire to possess anything at all, you cannot have your treasure in God alone."

But when we seek Him for Himself and find Him, we will often find, surprisingly, that those other things which we were so concerned about before have been "added unto us." God wants us to experience freedom and to have liberty, but He knows that the only true freedom is in experiential union with Him. He is the only free One; He is the only real One. "... where the Spirit of the Lord is, there is liberty" (2 Corinthians 3:17).

10

HEAVEN AND HELL – WHAT ARE THEY?

"Whom have I in heaven but thee?"

Psalms 73:25

Two basic reasons prevail today for why people wish to be Christians. Some people "accept Christ" primarily because they wish to escape their concept of hell, while others are motivated by a desire to know God. The first attitude is usually motivated by the self's understanding of heaven and hell, while the second comes from a truer understanding in the Spirit.

Many of us begin our Christian life for the first reason, the fear of some kind of hell. This is not really so shameful, because this fear does give us a start. Hell is, after all, to be avoided at all costs. But the self envisions heaven as a place that would be comfortable for it, and hell as a place that would be uncomfortable for it. And great consternation arises when the self (in mind) "realizes" that life in heaven can only be obtained at the cost of itself. Hence, it can find no real refuge in either heaven or hell.

When our interest is originally in escaping the discomforts of hell, we are surprised when we discover the truth; that eternal life costs us the very thing we were, by becoming a Christian, trying to gratify in the first place. In the beginning we did not realize this, because we did not yet recognize the illusory self as the source of all our problems.

The being that has found its substance in God looks for a place where, regardless of self's needs, it will be eternally united with God. This is the true heaven.

But the self-centered mind looks for a place where it will not be denied its wants and needs. It equates such a place with heaven. It labels as *hell* that place which would deny it or be contrary to its demands. The self will try meticulously to avoid such a place.

If God is the keeper of heaven, self concludes, then it would possibly be worth going through the momentary discomforts of religious duties, etc., in order to avoid a hell that would be eternal torture. To many, this is the sum of Christianity; a set of actions which they would prefer not to do, but which they dare not do without.

Many feel that they must go to church each Sunday just in case God is real after all. Then, they feel, they would have done what was required. Some also feel that, by learning certain spiritual concepts and principles, they can lead a more righteous life. By using what they think is God's own secrets and laws, they think to manipulate Him, thus getting His "blessings."

As these kinds of people are in the majority, many preachers who have no true knowledge of God themselves try to make their churches more accommodating to them. They organize sensitivity groups, encounter groups, games, movies, panel discussions, "exciting moves of the Spirit," etc., in order to show that the church isn't such a useless place after all. Often the most "successful" pastor is the one who can make his church the most interesting and profitable, while he assures his congregation that they are fulfilling their obligation to God.

Paul warned Timothy that in the last days there would be men having a form of godliness, but denying the power of it (*see* Timothy 3:5). That means that they would have an appearance of *true* religion, but deny the cross, which Paul states is the power of God (1 Corinthians 1:18).

These churches may even heavily emphasize holiness. The Pharisees, after all, made that their major point, also. Some may preach love and peace; some may even display what they think are spiritual gifts. Yes, we do need love, holiness, and the spiritual gifts, but Jesus said, "Many will say to me in that day, Lord, Lord, have we not prophesied in thy name? And in thy name have cast out devils? And in thy name done many wonderful works? And then will I profess unto them, I never *knew* you: depart from me, ye that work iniquity" (Matthew 7:22, 23).

It is possible to preach and teach of "deeper life spiritual principles," and to have all the "right" doctrine, and to discuss profound philosophical truths, and yet never know Him.

Some may be inclined to think that coming to Jesus is like going to the box office to get a ticket for the show. For them, Jesus is where they stop to get a ticket for heaven. They would rather not come to Him at all, because of the time and cost involved, but the show is reported to be well worth the ticket price.

The disastrous thing about this attitude is that Jesus is essentially all that there is to heaven. Those who view Him as the momentary inconvenience before the fun will be greatly disappointed. Yes, He is the way to the Father, but His purpose was to reveal the Father. God the Father is just more of the same, you might say.

Those who do not want Jesus would not like God the Father and heaven either. All of the kingdom is the same. In the words of the above analogy, there is nothing at the show that was not already at the box office.

Often we do not desire to come to Christ solely for Himself because we have a false, self-made picture, not only of heaven, but also of Christ. Out of love He methodically, piece by piece, destroys. that false self's picture we have of Him. Sometimes this can seem quite alarming, because we feel that *He* is being destroyed. But He is not being destroyed; our false picture of Him is simply being torn down.

We usually fight and kick against the destruction of our false picture. We desperately cling to the shattered remnants of our "Jesus." Some people continue to clutch tightly their illusions, even though they are shattered and useless. In this way they succeed at avoiding reality (and God) completely.

If this tearing-down process happens to us, we might presume that we will now find a true picture of Jesus to replace the one He destroyed. But in this attitude we persist in trying to see Him through our false self. This is impossible. Our efforts will only bring us nothing, or worse yet, more deception.

We are meant to see Him *by faith,* in the Spirit. We are meant to worship Him in spirit and in truth (*see* John 4:23, 24). "Wherefore henceforth know we no man after the flesh: yea, though we have known Christ after the flesh, yet now henceforth know we him no more". (2 Corinthians 5:16). He desires to reveal Himself to us in this new, higher way in the Spirit.

So we find that heaven is not an escape *for* the self. It is freedom *from* the self, from its pleasures as well as its pains, its good as well as its bad. "And to all He said, If anyone wishes to be a follower of mine, he must leave self behind; day after day he must take up his cross, and come with me. Whoever cares for his own safety is lost, but if a man will let himself be lost for my sake, that man is safe. What will a man gain by winning the whole world, at the cost of his true self?" (Luke 9:23-25 NEB). Christ's desire is for us to know Him, and His love will overcome all our illusions.

The Timeless Kingdom

We are inclined to think of eternity as beginning sometime in the future. While it may be true that we have not yet entered fully into it by our natural perception in time, we are nonetheless in it (positionally). Eternity has no beginning and no end. He cannot start sometime in the future, thus it must already be. It is not unending time; it is timelessness. Seeing it from our point of view in time, though, we visualize it as stretching into the infinite *past* as well as the infinite future.

The point of this is that the kingdom of God already *is*. We need not, indeed we should not, sit back and wait for it to come in the future. Since we know that it already is, we Christians can begin to live in it *now,* by faith, counting on it. It is inevitable, a certainty, that some day it will be seen by all. Jesus said, "As you go proclaim that the kingdom of Heaven has arrived" (Matthew 10:7 PHILLIPS). "Who [God] hath delivered us from the power of darkness, and hath translated us into the kingdom of his dear Son" (Colossians 1:13).

The fact that all do not see the eternal kingdom openly and manifestly does not mean that it does not yet exist. The kingdom already exists in the eternal now, if not yet by our natural sight or in our viewpoint of time. Paul says that we have already been seated with Christ in the heavenlies (*see* Ephesians 2:6). We are in Christ now. That means that our real life transcends time and is unchangeable. Even though we do not yet, with our natural faculties, see ourselves there, we can count on it as a fact. It is true in the eternal now, which includes past, present, and future, and includes the beginning and the end.

It is not so important that the kingdom has not yet been shown to all in time, because the fact that it exists does not change. Positionally we are in the kingdom. By relying upon this as the fact, rather than waiting to perceive it with our senses, we can begin to find it true in our experience, just as Jesus did. The fact that it is true will not automatically make it true in our experience; we must acknowledge it as being so in the kingdom, and rely upon it. Then our experience becomes one with the facts. We walk in the kingdom of God.

Jesus is the Lamb slain from the foundations of the world. The prophets of old counted on Him in type and shadow, even though He had not then been crucified in time. Regardless of its point in time, the Crucifixion was a fact in eternity. So it is with all things; they only change in time, but in the kingdom they remain constant.

We can rely on things in the kingdom to remain the same forever. This means not just for the future, but for the past also, as the kingdom is timeless. We already have peace, rest, liberty from sin, and communion with God in Christ in the eternal now. By relying upon this as fact, we can also know it in time, right now. After all, isn't that what it's all about?

Since Christ, rather than our old ego or self, represents us now, it becomes increasingly more natural for the soul to follow Him, as He is what is true of us. We are included with Him now and forever. It is not a matter of denying reality and attempting to live contrary to the truth; exactly the opposite is true. We lived contrary to reality when our self was representing us and we were under the law. But it is a fact, the very truth, that Christ is our true life and that we live in Him.

When we believe Christ to be our life, we have all that is His, *His past* as well as His present and future. He is the eternal I AM; when we are in Him, all is new for us, *even our past*. He took *all* of us on the cross with Him, and in exchange gave us His all. All that is ours is Christ's, and all that is Christ's is ours, through the grace of the abounding, unsearchable goodness and mercy of God.

If we have been concerned about the effects of our sins upon others; we will be glad to know that, through the cross of Jesus Christ, those effects do not even exist in the eternal now. Not only has He taken upon Himself our sins, but also the effects of our sins upon others, and the effect of their sins upon us. In Scripture we can relate this to the Jewish scapegoat (Leviticus 16:20-26).

It is also tiresome and useless to entertain imaginings about other people who might be unkind and unfair to us, and to worry about events that might cheat us of our "rights" or cause our flesh discomfort. These worries and imaginings are all of and for the old nature; they simply nurture self-pity. In the kingdom, the eternal now, none of those things exist. There is no justice in the world system. We lose our freedom if we expect it. Is our thought life in the kingdom or in the world, the old creature or the new creature? Our body may be in the world, but we are *of* the kingdom. The "me" we think we are doesn't count for us, count on Christ. That which does not conform to the kingdom is only wood, hay, and stubble, fit for the fire. Imaginations are temporary and passing. They are separate from the real us, and not important to us in the least. We are not our imaginations. We are one with Christ.

Isaiah has a clue for us, and gives us a glimpse of the eternal now. "For, behold, I create new heavens and a new earth: and the former shall not be remembered, nor come into mind" (Isaiah 65:17). We also find a little later, "For as the new heavens and the new earth, which I will make, shall remain before me, saith the Lord, so shall your seed and your name remain" (Isaiah 66:22). That is for us in Christ.

In the New Testament Peter confirms this, saying, "Nevertheless, we, according to his promise, look for new heavens and a new earth, wherein dwelleth righteousness" (2 Peter 3:13). He says earlier, "But the day of the Lord will come as a thief in the night; in the which the heavens shall pass away with a great noise, and the elements shall melt with fervent heat; the earth also and the works that are therein shall be burned up. Seeing then that all these things shall be dissolved, what manner of persons ought ye to be in all holy conversation and godliness" (2 Peter 3:10, II).

Peter is telling us not to waste our time on the things that are not included in the kingdom, that are apart from Christ. For those of us who are in Christ, there is great rejoicing that all is done away with which is outside of Christ. Indeed, with Christ's Crucifixion, it has already passed away, and some day will be seen to do so manifestly in time.

This will be terrible for those without Christ, because they will have lost everything. But for those in Christ, there will be much rejoicing. Everything for which the soul was made sorry shall be removed forever, and everything which the soul counted upon and looked forward to shall be theirs forever. On the day of the Lord's return all of this will be shown openly, and there will be no more questions as to reality and the truth. It will be made clear to all, saved or unsaved.

11

The Disciple Whom Jesus Loved

"I have loved thee with an everlasting love."

Jeremiah 31:3

In the Gospel of John the author often refers to himself as "the disciple whom Jesus loved" (John 19:26). At first glance, John might appear to be rather presumptuous and inclined towards writing more highly of himself than of those around him. But as we see and begin to discover for ourselves what the love of God is like, we can better appreciate John's statement.

Rather than referring to a particular high quality in himself, John was only recognizing the quality of the love of Jesus. John was not impressed by his own lovableness, but was instead relying on the free flow of Jesus' infinite love for him. That phrase used by John referred not so much to himself as to Jesus, and the type of love that Jesus had. John simply recognized that love and allowed Jesus to love him.

Many times we refuse the love of Christ because we recognize that we are not lovable. Peter, when he first met Jesus, said, "Depart from me, for I am a sinful man"

(Luke 5:8). We may not outwardly recognize our humility, but still we envision our guilt as much greater than the infinite, abounding love of God.

We then cannot appreciate the value of the blood of Jesus to cleanse us of our sins, and the value of the cross of Jesus to deal with what we are. Thus we are limited in receiving God's love for us. God does not love us any less or stop loving us for this, but **we** are often unable to recognize and receive His love.

John recognized that the kind of love Jesus had transcended John himself; it was greater than the flaws of John, greater than the sins of John, greater than John's own lack of lovableness. We, too, can begin to count on, not our lovableness, but the kind of love that Jesus has. God doesn't love you for what you do or don't do. He loves you because you are His.

As we have learned, God cannot and does not love the person we thought we were, "me," and try as we will we simply could not convince ourselves that God could really hate sin and still love us. For while we identified with self we *were* sin. If receiving God's love is a problem in our lives, we can be sure that an unclear perception of the cross is at the bottom of it. It always is. God loves our soul, not the false self. That's precisely why He counted us in Christ, so that you, as John did, can rest on Jesus' breast. He is the One who assumed our own shameful imaginary self and the deeds associated upon Himself and bore the loss of God for the sin we were, so that we could be reconciled to the Father in the identity of His own righteousness.

And soon we will begin to realize that we, too, are "the disciple whom Jesus loves." We can enter into the love of God, and can give the glory for it to Him. This is divine love, agape.

In order to do this we must receive Jesus' love apart from any merit of our own. It is much easier for the false self to receive a gift of which we feel worthy than one which we know we do not deserve at all. When in our hearts we truly see the type of person that we are as the false self, we know that we do not deserve the love of God in the least.

And we know that He knows us even better than we ourselves. Because of our own complete lack of lovableness we must depend utterly upon God's infinite capacity to love. So it is only in this supreme mortification, the complete abasement of ourselves, that we receive the totally undeserved, unearned love of God.

Once that is done, however, and we recognize the boundless capability of Christ to love us, we find a most solid base upon which to rest. This base also becomes the springboard of our own love towards God. As we decrease, He increases in our sight.

God's love is not merely toleration for us, nor is it a general love for all mankind. He loves us singly as much as all His creations together. We need not even see ourselves as one among many, for through the body and blood of Jesus Christ, we are as a favorite child of God the Father.

We may receive as much love and devotion as a favorite child, not needing to stand in the background because of being less than another. When we receive God's love in this way, we will find immediately that our hard hearts melt. Our whole attitude changes, and we find ourselves loving Christ in a way that we could never love Him before.

This is because we are resting upon the solid foundation of *His* love, rather than our own lovableness or ability to love Him. We have our ability to love only by receiving God's love first. "We love him, because he first loved us" (1 John 4:19). We might even say that we become lovable only by first receiving God's love.

Christianity is a funny business this way. Our inclination is to feel that by loving God and others first we can get Him to love us, or that by being lovable we can win His love. But He turns the whole thing upside down and inside out; and, we find, we are much happier for it.

John was not able to lay his head upon Christ's breast because he knew that Christ preferred him above the rest of the disciples. Indeed, Christ loved them all in a depth that we cannot even measure. John simply *acknowledged* Christ's love for him and responded to it.

He allowed Christ to love him, and received that love by resting on Christ. This picture of John leaning upon Jesus' breast is very symbolic of the way that we are to rest upon Christ and His love. We can count on, and even assume, His unchanging love for us.

We may find it hard to imagine that God does love us, but that is because we might still be identifying with "me," the old nature that was crucified with Christ. God's love reaches us because He identifies us with Christ and loves the new creature *in Christ* because He loves Christ. Then we don't have to imagine anything, we *know* that He loves Christ-His beloved Son in whom He is well pleased – and if we know that Christ is our new life, God's love becomes a *fact* to us in the present.

This type of love relationship with God is not reserved for those who are "spiritual," or those who are always doing good things in the church, or those whom we think God would be likely to love. God's love, even in this deep way, this profound way, is for "whosoever will" (Luke 9:24; Revelation 22:17).

Even with our own children we find that we are more able to share love with those who desire and receive our love. We may love and desire another child as much; but if he does not desire to receive that love, we will not force it on him. It would not really be love then.

But there is so much power in the cross of Christ, that even if one thinks he has no desire for God's love the cross can even produce that. Such was Peter's reaction when he said, “Depart from me; for I am a sinful man” (Luke 5:8). But the marvelous fact is that through the cross we have been removed from the unacceptable sinner and miraculously placed in the Beloved Son. When we realize that good news, desire for God fairly abounds, because now it is *possible* to be loved by Him. Before, it was so impossible that desire for Him seemed like useless torture. Now it is a blessed reality.

For “the disciple whom Jesus loved,” this was just the beginning. Upon receiving that love, he could love Jesus more, and in turn receive even more of the love that God had for him in Christ Jesus. And he could go on later to find out and to write that, “God is love” (1 John 4:8).

The Bride Of Christ

When God's Holy Spirit begins to illuminate our understanding of the exchanged life, we begin to see that all Christians are indeed one positionally, if not experientially. We are all one not just figuratively, but literally. “For we being many are one bread, and one body” (1 Corinthians 10:17).

When we all look to the same Jesus for our one shared life, we see this as already accomplished in the kingdom. Instead of having to initiate ecumenical movements, or trying to mesh people's natural minds in agreement, we can simply look once again to what God has already accomplished in Christ.

We cannot experience this oneness through organizations, politics, or any other way, except by faith. The fallen natures of men can never be united as Christ's body. Men may be united in a cause through man's effort, but the motives for unification are invariably for self-preservation or self-gain.

Men have always been able to maintain a semblance of unity if the goal is of sufficient value to self. No matter how altruistic the motives for the cause may seem, they inevitably are veiled desires for personal gain. The result is then necessarily political rather than spiritual.

We are not one because we belong to the same group of people, or because we give mental assent to the same understanding. True oneness in Christ will include agreement in understanding, etc., but it is the *result,* not the *cause,* of spiritual union with Christ. *Because* we are sharing the one mystical life, we will find ourselves of one mind in one accord.

The natural man's way is the other way around. If people can come upon a commonly acceptable set of creeds, he reasons, then they will be one. The old creature always wants to do things backwards. He causes himself a lot of useless work trying to counterfeit what

God has already accomplished. But man finds that hard to believe, let alone understand.

The reason for all this confusion is that we really cannot share and experience this oneness in Christ's life until we have first accepted Christ's death as our death, also. Yes – it's the cross again! The nature of man always attempts to avoid the cross. He tries to do this by copying in the flesh what God has already accomplished in the Spirit. Thus he thinks that by doing so he can bypass the cross. But that is the spirit of antichrist, and is false. If we could only see this, many, many organizations, ambitions, plans, fears, and frustrations would fall by the wayside.

We are not made one as the result of agreeing with one another. That's law. We will agree *because* we see we are already one in Christ. That's grace!

"For the love of Christ constraineth us; because we thus judge, that if one died for all, then were all dead: And that he died for all, that they who live should not henceforth live unto themselves, but unto him which died for them, and rose again. Wherefore henceforth know we no man after the flesh; yea, though we have known Christ after the flesh, yet now henceforth know we him no more. Therefore if any man be in Christ, he is a new creature: old things are passed away; behold, all things are become new. And all things are of God,

who hath reconciled us to himself by Jesus Christ, and hath given to us the ministry of reconciliation."

2 Corinthians 5:14-18

Paul's order in the Scripture which was just quoted is very important. In verse 14 he explains how Christ's love will control us if we see and count on the fact that we share *one* death in Jesus. Then, and only then, can we share His *one* life (verse 15). Our carnal motives for knowing people are ruled out, because the carnal creation was nullified on the cross (verses 16, 17).

If we recognize Christ's resurrection life and count on it to save us, then we must also identify our brothers and sisters with that one resurrection life. Our new nature is Christ, and He is in God. This is also true for our brothers and sisters, whether they fully realize it and manifest it or not.

Thus we have an entirely new way to relate to one another: not through common likes and dislikes of the flesh, etc., but through our literal positional oneness in Christ. Then we will naturally care for one another, just as one part of our physical body cares spontaneously for another part because they share the same biological identity. Just as the physical body does this instinctively, so will we spontaneously love one another as we see our true oneness in Christ.

Many give in expectation of return. Agape gives, and gives spontaneously, requiring nothing in return. Since we have God, we have everything worthwhile, and we can give with no thought or need of repayment. We need not worry about helping others; as we behold the love of Christ, we will begin to do so without consciously thinking about it. Our help will then be natural and spontaneous and without effort. Even more important, it will be of real benefit to others, not just display.

We will turn from pushing “right doctrine” to simply sharing, in Christ's love and power, God's provision and desire for His personal reconciliation with every soul (verse 15).

This life of liberty and fellowship with God is for us to live and share with those who desire it. We need not expect, require, assume, or depend on others to live, or even desire, this life. Our liberty depends, not upon anyone else, but only upon Christ who is our life. Requiring this of others will only lead to disappointment and bondage. We don't need to project our ideals on others, even if they seem worthy, for we will be imposing an image upon them. To do so is not fair to them. We can count them as also being in Christ, and let them be and love them as Christ. “Henceforth know we no man after the flesh: but after the Spirit” (2 Corinthians 5:16). Live *with* others, but not *upon* them. We will then share our peace and joy and liberty and communion with God.

Christ said, "My sheep will know my voice," and "All those that are mine will come to me." When Christ manifests His life through us, He will draw His other sheep to Himself. "... if I be lifted up [I] will draw all men unto me" (John 12:32). This is a crucified and resurrected life. Christ's death works in us, that His life might be known to others. Let me leave you with one last conundrum: The asker is the answer.

God's design is not just to bring a group of individual Christians into their own individual kingdoms of God. If we stop at this, we miss the whole point of God's plan for mankind.

God desires a bride for His Son. Christ's bride, though, will not be brought into a carnal unity through fear of punishment or hope of reward, or indeed by any rules or regulations. God desires for His Son a bride united in His Son's own body and *love*. As was with the first Adam, Christ's bride was also created of Him while He slept. But Christ, in death, endured the very forces of hell while she, Christ's bride, was formed of His own flesh and blood, and He has given her His name. Oh, what kind of love must this be?

This kind of love is in Spirit and in truth (*see* John 4:23, 24). It binds one to another as Christ's body and bride, and embraces Christ, the Groom, as the head of the body. Get ready, for the marriage supper is beginning. Let us put everything else aside to come and enter into God's love.

As this book comes to an end, it is hoped that it has been instrumental in establishing the reader firmly and solidly in the kingdom of God as was the intention at the beginning. After passing through the narrow way that leadeth into life, we find a wide open and infinitely huge kingdom to explore, as big as God Himself. After all, He is the kingdom and we are in Him by Christ. It is not this writer's intention to leave the reader now, for as he will perceive, he is not alone; for there he will find not only this writer, but every other Christian who ever walked the earth or ever will, and best of all, God Himself.

EPILOGUE

This book is intended as a statement of the grace of God through Jesus Christ; it is to show the means God has provided for us to experientially know Him.

"Though being many, we are one bread and one body." And we can all begin to discover, live in, and share the kingdom in our own family, church, and neighborhood, right where we are. The kingdom of God has arrived!

"...for it is in Him in whom we live and move and have our being." (Acts 17:28)

This book now closes, that another book (the Bible) may open.

REFERENCE

All Scripture quotations, unless otherwise identified are from the King James Version of the Bible.

Scripture quotations identified as PHILLIPS are from The New Testament in Modern English translated by J.B Phillips, Copyright J.P Phillips, 1958.

Scripture quotations identified as NEB are from The New English Bible. © The Delegates of the Oxford University Press and the Syndics of the Cambridge University Press 1961 and 1970.

Scripture quotations identified as LB are from the Living Bible, Copyright © 1971 by Tyndale House Publishers, Wheaton, Illinois 60187. All Rights reserved.

Scripture quotations identified as AMPLIFIED are from The Amplified New Testament, © The Lockman Foundation 1958.

About The Author

Galen Sharp is a professional artist and author. He has explored and studied the teachings of the Bible in depth over the course of his life. This exploration lead to an intuitive insight, which shed a whole new light on the teachings of the Bible. This intuitive insight is genuine inner spiritual awakening. This spiritual awakening is often referred to by Christian Mystics as "Union with God." Galen's own intuitive awakening revealed to him that in fact Oneness with God is our natural state. Galen felt drawn to share this simple and direct yet profound intuitive understanding of our Inherent Oneness with God with others. His own intuitive recognition of our inherent Oneness with God, informs his writing in this book as he paves the way to begin to see the teachings of the Bible in a whole new light.

Made in United States
North Haven, CT
23 August 2022